Praise for *Friending*

"As we've come to expect from Lynne Baab, inside *Friending* are thoughtful questions, fascinating research and excellent biblical analysis. I found her discussion on the new wave of technology and how this impacts relationships quite illuminating. This would be an excellent book for small groups to discuss and for anyone who wants help in how to be a faithful friend—to God, to our families and to our circle of friends."

Rebecca Manley Pippert, author of *Out of the Saltshaker and Into the World*

"Lynne Baab offers interesting reflection on the changing nature of friendship in a networked society, where relationships are increasingly cultivated and sustained through social media. Using engaging real-life examples she asks important questions about how friendships may be shaped in certain directions when mediated through technology and the potential spiritual consequences of these interactions. Importantly the book calls readers to personally consider the intentionality and motivations behind their own friendship practices to uncover what values they stem from and the social world they may cultivate."

Heidi Campbell, author of *Exploring Religious Community Online*

"Friends are so important to me! But today there are more forces pushing us apart—as well as new media to bring us together—than ever before in history. Lynne Baab explores a world of options and encourages us to redevelop the art of friendship for a new era. This book is full of practical tools, winsome stories and keen insights. I'm hooked."

Steve Hayner, president, Columbia Theological Seminary

Lynne M. Baab

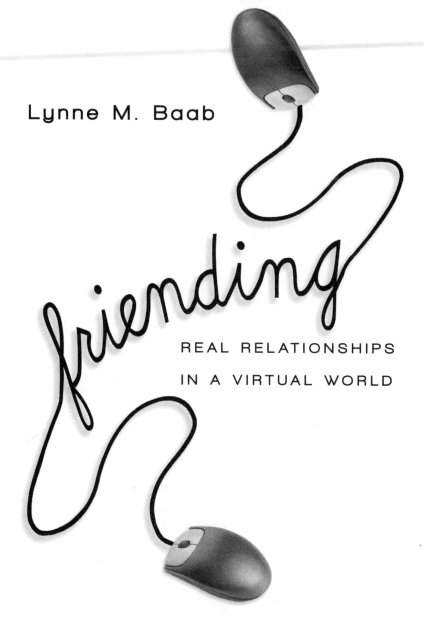

friending

REAL RELATIONSHIPS

IN A VIRTUAL WORLD

IVP Books

An imprint of InterVarsity Press
Downers Grove, Illinois

InterVarsity Press
P.O. Box 1400, Downers Grove, IL 60515-1426
World Wide Web: www.ivpress.com
E-mail: email@ivpress.com

InterVarsity Press® is the book-publishing division of InterVarsity Christian Fellowship/USA®, a
movement of students and faculty active on campus at hundreds of universities, colleges and schools
of nursing in the United States of America, and a member movement of the International Fellowship
of Evangelical Students. For information about local and regional activities, write Public Relations
Dept., InterVarsity Christian Fellowship/USA, 6400 Schroeder Rd., P.O. Box 7895, Madison, WI
53707-7895, or visit the IVCF website at <www.intervarsity.org>.

While all stories in this book are true, some names and identifying information in this book have
been changed to protect the privacy of the individuals involved. All stories about friendships are told
by permission.

Design: Cindy Kiple
Images: Luis Carlos Torres/iStockphoto

ISBN 978-0-8308-3419-8

Printed in the United States of America ∞

Library of Congress Cataloging-in-Publication Data

Baab, Lynne M.
  Friending: real relationships in a virtual world / Lynne M. Baab.
     p. cm.
  Includes bibliographical references.
  ISBN 978-0-8308-3419-8 (pbk.: alk. paper)
  1. Friendship—Religious aspects—Christianity. 2. Online social
networks—Religious aspects—Christianity. I. Title.
  BV4647.F7B33 2011
  241'.6762—dc22

                                                                    2010052960

| P | 18 | 17 | 16 | 15 | 14 | 13 | 12 | 11 | 10 | 9 | 8 | 7 | 6 | 5 | 4 | 3 | 2 | 1 |
| Y | 26 | 25 | 24 | 23 | 22 | 21 | 20 | 19 | 18 | 17 | 16 | 15 | 14 | 13 | 12 | 11 |

CONTENTS

ACKNOWLEDGMENTS
AND DEDICATION

So many people talked to me about friendship, in person, in emails, on the phone and on Facebook. So many people sent me links to online articles on friendship and clipped out articles from magazines and newspapers. A list of names would fill this page and more, and I am indebted to all of you. I couldn't have written this book without you. May you enjoy rich and fruitful friendships.

Special thanks go to three people. Kelly Pearson interviewed more than a dozen of her friends for me, giving me lots of stories and definitions of friendship. Thank you, Kelly. My colleagues Paul Trebilco and Murray Rae looked over parts of the manuscript for theological and biblical accuracy, and gave me ideas to increase the theological depth. Thank you, Paul and Murray.

My mother, my brother, my husband and my sons have talked with me about friendship many, many times. All of you have helped me understand friendship and grow in it. Loving thanks to you all. My editor at InterVarsity Press, Dave Zimmerman, shaped this book in numerous ways. Thank you, Dave.

This book is dedicated to all my friends, past and present. Thank you for the support, encouragement, affection and love you have given me. You have been an anchor, a flame of light and a warm quilt in my life. I can't begin to imagine how impoverished my life would be without you.

1

REAL RELATIONSHIPS

*A friend is someone you can rely on through thick and thin, who under-
stands you, and who would tell you the cold hard truth. A friend is someone
with similar interests who you want to spend time with. A friend understands
your jokes and makes you smile.*
—A definition from a group of teenagers, ages sixteen to nineteen

*Two are better than one, because they have a good reward for their toil. For
if they fall, one will lift up the other; but woe to one who is alone and falls
and does not have another to help.*
—Ecclesiastes 4:9-10

The light from a clear blue sky flooded my home office as I
turned on my computer. My husband was eating breakfast, and
the cheerful clinking of dishes from the other side of the house,
coupled with the slanting morning sunshine on the trees outside
my window, made me feel lighthearted and optimistic about the day.

I found a handful of new emails, one of them from my editor at
InterVarsity Press. He and I had been discussing the possibility
that I would write a book on friendship as a spiritual practice in
this electronic age. When I saw his email, I wondered if the edito-
rial committee had met to discuss my proposal.

I opened the email. Great news! They wanted me to write the
book.

I wrote back, telling him I was delighted and mentioning one detail I'd thought of since we last corresponded. I closed his email and found one from my brother, Mark, responding to an article about golf I had sent him the day before and mentioning his son, Ross, who works in a hotel.

> Hi there Lynne. That was a funny article you sent me yesterday. We're feeling pretty happy here because Ross just got a promotion. He'll have a regular shift at the front desk rather than filling in as needed. It will mean full-time hours for him.

I wrote a quick email back to Mark.

> Give Ross my congratulations. And you can congratulate me, too. You're the first person to know I'm going to be writing a book on friendship in the Facebook age. I just got an email from my editor and I'm really, really happy.

Mark happened to be online and wrote back right away.

> Great news, Lynne. Here's a story for your book. Ross found out that the position had opened up at work because of Facebook. The guy who was fired from the position did some venting on Facebook, so Ross knew he could apply. Ross heard the news first on Facebook, at home, on his day off.

I wrote back to Mark, joking about the situation and its significance for what I wanted to say in the book. As I wrote, I pondered the fact that Mark was writing from his office in Oregon, while I live in New Zealand. My brother and I—seven thousand miles apart—were having this conversation about my book and about communication, while my husband was peacefully eating breakfast only two rooms away from me, not yet knowing I was going to write the book.

Is something wrong with this picture? I wondered. Not everyone can say her husband is her best friend, but I can. Was I slighting my best friend, who happened to be in close physical proximity to me, to have this online discussion with my brother, who was on the other side of the world? Or was this simply a normal aspect of life today?

The new communication technologies of the past two to three decades have shrunk our world. People far away are present to us with an immediacy that was unimaginable only thirty years ago. What are "real" relationships in this new context? What are the characteristics of healthy, life-giving friendships in today's world? What choices and skills are necessary to navigate these new realities?

It's a bit daunting to undertake the writing of this book, because so many people have such vehement opinions about these questions. I have read their forceful views online in blogs and newspapers, and in print as well. Opinions on the subject of friendship today vary tremendously. On the one hand, many writers have expressed their passionate opinion—usually based on their own experience—that the many new communication technologies facilitate friendships in fresh and exciting ways. All these new ways of communicating are helpful, they say, in mitigating against the busy schedules and scattering of loved ones that can make relationships challenging in our time.

On the other hand, many other writers use words like *faux*, *pseudo* or *imitation* to describe friendships today, particularly friendships with a significant Internet component. They believe we have exchanged meaningful and intimate face-to-face friendships for impersonal, superficial online connections. People can't talk to each other with any depth these days, they assert, and as a result relationships are impoverished.

How will I navigate a path in the midst of these strong and heartfelt opinions?

I'm also feeling daunted at the challenge of writing this book, because putting friendship under a microscope seems potentially dangerous. What if it damages my own friendships? My friends are one of the most precious gifts in my life. They have supported, encouraged and affirmed me. When times have been hard, they have listened to my endless worries and complaints. I am thrilled at the diversity of gifts and personalities among my friends, and I feel awed when I think about their commitments and expertise in so many areas. To have a window into their thoughts and priorities is a great privilege, and to be a part of their lives challenges me to be my best self.

To analyze something almost always changes it. Scary.

But I do want to write this book. I've been thinking about friendships and how they work since I was a child. We moved almost a dozen times in my first fifteen years, so from an early age I had to give attention to the question of how to find and care for friends. I believe the basic skills of friendship remain constant, and I want to write about those skills, exploring the way they apply in the global, frenetic, digitally connected world today.

I see friendship as a spiritual practice, a place where we live out the things we believe in. Friendship is a space where our values and commitments take flesh. This is true for people of any kind of religious commitment and for people who have none.

For the sake of readers who have a Christian faith commitment or an interest in seeing the connections between the Christian faith and friendship today, I want to discuss the ways friendship with God overlaps with our other friendships. This very best Friend can teach us a lot about how to relate to others, guiding us, empowering us and giving us the confidence and peace that undergird healthy friendships. The many biblical passages about relationships are just as relevant in the online world and in our homes, neighborhoods and workplaces today as they were in dusty Palestine two thousand years ago.

RESOURCES FOR THIS BOOK

In preparation for writing this book, I interviewed dozens of people ranging in age from twelve to eighty-five. They said fantastic and fascinating things about friendship, and you'll hear their voices throughout the book. You'll also hear the voices of some of my closest family members, with whom I've been discussing friendship all my life.

My mother, now in her mid-eighties, has been a powerful model of friendship for me. She has a small group of very close friends and a whopping circle of other friends and acquaintances. She is always open to making a new friend at church, at her golf club, in her neighborhood or in the wider community. She invites people over for meals, writes cards and notes, makes phone calls, sends emails and shares photos online. My father died several years ago, and my mother now goes on trips with her friends. She is always very conscious of those friends she hasn't seen for a while, and she makes contact when too much time has elapsed. Mom has said to me many times, "You have to work at friendships. If you don't, they wither." She lives out her commitment to her friends every day of her life.

My brother, in his fifties, is another valuable conversation partner with me on the subject of friendships. Mark has a tight circle of close friends, and he has made many intentional choices to provide support to them over the years. He works hard to be faithful to his family, so he limits his time with friends, but he never neglects them. Every Friday after work, he gathers with his buddies to drink beer and swap stories for a couple of hours. He might play golf or squash with one or two of them during the week as well. Once a year he spends a weekend in Reno with his circle of local friends, expanded to include his two closest friends from high school, who live a couple of hundred miles away. And once a year this same group of his local and high-school friends spends five days together skiing. My brother exemplifies a wonderful balance of work, family and friends, and he models careful, intentional thinking about friendships.

My two sons have also stimulated my thinking about friendships. My younger son, in his late twenties, nurtures a wide circle of friends strewn all over the world. He keeps up with them through blog posts and Facebook, and by texting on his cell phone, emailing, Skyping and visiting. My older son, in his early thirties, has nurtured a deep friendship with his wife, and he also stays in close touch with his childhood best friend. He uses Facebook, email and phone calls to stay in contact with his wider circle of friends. He Skypes frequently with my husband, his father, who he considers to be one of his closest friends.

TWO VIEWS ABOUT COMMUNICATION TECHNOLOGIES

My sons represent two significant viewpoints about friendships and new communication technologies. My younger son believes that this is the best time in human history for friendships, simply because of the many options for staying connected. "I can be on a business trip in New York City," he said, "and I see something in a shop window that reminds me of a friend in Europe. I can pull out my cell phone and flip him a text message. Or later that day I can send him an email or instant-message with him online. I can post something on Facebook or on my blog that I know that friend will like."

All those varied forms of contact, he believes, make it possible for us to begin from a point of connection rather than distance when we see friends face-to-face. He notes that the variety of ways to connect provides options for people with different communication preferences to find one way or a few ways to stay in touch that suits them. He is convinced that all this makes friendship alive and vibrant in our time.

My older son enjoys the variety of ways to stay connected as well, but he has concerns about them and is generally less optimistic than his brother about their benefits. He believes we are shaped by the communication technologies we use the most. He is concerned about the brevity of cell-phone text messages, updates on social-networking websites and even emails. He believes they nurture glib and flippant communication styles that damage meaningful communication and inhibit depth in relationships, particularly over the long haul. He said,

Have you ever noticed that the actors in movies from the 1950s all seem to talk in rich, plummy tones? They sound like radio announcers, which is understandable because they all listened to hours and hours of radio during the Depression and World War II. Their communication style was shaped by what they heard so often. In the same way, people who watch a lot of TV seem to talk in sound bites and expect everyone to be beautiful. Just watch. People who send a lot of text messages and post short, offhand comments on Twitter or Facebook are going to be shaped by that style of communicating.

Scholars call his viewpoint "technological determinism."[1] This school of thought asserts that the communication technologies we use determine the way we use them; each communication technology has its limits, and those limits shape the messages and ultimately shape the person sending the messages as well. Much of the negative discourse about online communication comes from the technological determinist perspective. Because cell-phone texting and most Internet communication eliminate nonverbal cues that convey emotion, technological determinists are deeply concerned that significant aspects of human communication are missing when certain communication technologies are used.

On the opposite end of the spectrum is the view that technologies are inherently neutral, that the content we put in them gives them form and meaning. My younger son's optimism about all the wonderful ways to stay connected today has some parallels with this "technology is neutral" way of thinking.

Heidi Campbell, a researcher who studies the way religious communities and individuals in them use new communication technologies, argues for a middle ground. She notes that people of faith—like everyone else—have always shaped different communication technologies to suit their own needs.[2] The printing press, telegraph, telephone, TV, movies, cell phones and now the Internet have been used strategically to meet the goals of organizations and individuals. She believes that any technology does not totally determine the way it is used. Her research indicates that people bring their own priorities, goals and passions to communication technologies and shape their use in unexpected ways. Yet, at the same time, she agrees that each form of communication encourages some styles of interaction and makes other styles more difficult. She believes that online communication is excellent for conveying information; however, depth, emotion and intimate connection are harder to convey online. Campbell believes, as I do, that nurturing deep relationships that have a significant online component requires intentionality and commitment.

Ultimately, where we land on the spectrum—of technological determinism versus technology as neutral—is not the most significant issue with respect to friendship. Communication technologies are what they are *and* they are what we make of them. Meanwhile, this book focuses on friendship: what friendship is and what we make of our friendships. It's my hope that this book will help you explore all sides of the spectrum and come out the other side with deeper, richer experiences of friendship in all its fullness.

Throughout this book, I will be referring to *social networking,* a way to describe websites designed for enabling people to connect to each other. As I write, Facebook and LinkedIn are the most popular forms of social networking—Facebook for personal relationships and LinkedIn for professional networks. Only a few of my interviewees use Twitter to keep up with their friends. Many of them use Twitter to follow famous people in their field or pop celebrities, and those who blog often post updates about their blogs on Twitter. Some of my interviewees used Bebo, MySpace or Friendster in the past, but they have switched to Facebook.

Because Facebook in particular was mentioned by the majority of my interviewees, Facebook will function in most of the stories in this book as a kind of case study for online social networking.

Online patterns of communication morph quickly, so I will refer to social networking instead of Facebook as often as possible so that the book will have relevance when Facebook declines in popularity and something else comes along.

In addition to social-networking websites, many other new forms of communication connect friends with each other. Many bloggers enjoy in-depth discussions with the people who respond to their blog posts. Photo-sharing websites, online discussion groups and websites for people with narrowly focused interests provide venues for meaningful connection. Skype—online video conferencing—is becoming increasingly common. Many people use instant messaging, and email remains popular. Sending text messages with a cell phone is a significant way of staying connected for many people. These and other communication options will undoubtedly continue to proliferate, and the kinds of intentionality and commitment discussed in this book will have relevance for the new, and as yet unknown, forms of connection as well.

CHANGING DEFINITIONS OF FRIENDSHIP

I asked several dozen people, ranging in age from late teens to late forties, whether the use of *friend* to refer to contacts on social-networking websites is changing the way they understand friendship. All of them said no.

A good number of people who responded to that question said that all their contacts on Facebook are people they already know fairly well or very well. So calling them friends is appropriate. The rest of the people who responded said that they have a variety of ways of referring to a Facebook friend who they do not know in person or do not know well enough to call a real friend. They might say "Facebook contact" or "someone I know on Facebook." One woman said that when she refers to friends, she usually uses some kind of modifier anyway: "friend from high school," "friend from work," or "Facebook friend" if she knows the person only from Facebook. Many of her friends from high

school and from work are also her friends on Facebook, but she
doesn't think of them that way because the connection is rooted
elsewhere in her life.

Online social networking has changed friendship vocabulary
in one notable way: the word *friend* has become a verb. To "friend"
someone is to request that they become a friend on a social-
networking website or to accept their request. To "defriend" is to
delete him or her as an online contact. In my interviews, no one
used *friend* or *defriend* as verbs for anything other than online actions. Perhaps in the years to come, *friend* or *defriend* as verbs will
also be used to refer to acts related to face-to-face friendship, but I
didn't hear anyone use the words that way.

As the title of this book indicates, I like some aspects of the
verb *friending*. I want to encourage discussion about the ways
friendship—online or offline—is like a verb. Being a friend involves significant actions of caring and commitment. The adage
"The only way to have a friend is to be a friend" is still profound
and true. Learning how to be a friend and engaging consistently
in actions that express friendship reflect the reality that friendship is more like a verb than a noun.

In this book I will argue that nurturing deep friendships in any
setting requires intentionality and commitment. Today's Western
lifestyle creates three major challenges to friendship: the online
component of so many relationships, the frantic pace of life, and
the scattering of family and friends to scattered locations. Never
before have so many people conducted so many of their relationships using such a wide range of technologies that includes cell
phones, computers, smartphones, gaming consoles connected to
the Internet and many other forms of technology. Never before has
the pace of life been so frantic, with electric light making day and
night irrelevant and with people racing around juggling a myriad
of commitments. And never before has mobility been so rampant,
resulting in families and friends dispersed to the four corners of
the world.

CONFIDENCE ABOUT FRIENDSHIP

Despite these challenges, most of the people I interviewed were confident they knew how to develop and nurture friendships. Many expressed frustration about the implications in their daily life of three obstacles mentioned above—the tendency of electronic communication to be impersonal, busy schedules and friends who live far away—but only a few expressed concerns that they don't really know how to go about making and keeping friends.

The generational patterns in the interviews were fascinating. Just about everyone with whom I spoke was concerned about someone else's use of technology in relationships, and those concerns were expressed in generational terms.

The people my age, in their fifties, told me they had learned how to nurture strong and healthy face-to-face friendships during all those years before computers. They expressed a lot of concern about people in their twenties and thirties, wondering if they'll be able to sustain marriage and parenting relationships, because they're so used to communicating using technology. The glib, brief and trivial nature of so much online communication might contribute to superficial relationships. Can people in their twenties and thirties have long, intimate conversations? Can they share their deepest feelings?

My two sons, in their late twenties and early thirties, as well as others their age whom I interviewed, are confident of their own ability to nurture intimate friendships. Several of them cited the many years of their childhood without cell phones or the Internet, saying they learned how to have close friends before the age of rampant electronic communication. However, these young adults expressed concern about teenagers: with the proliferation of such brief messages in text messages and online posts, will they be able to engage in the kind of deep conversations that nurture true friendships?

The dozen or so teenagers I interviewed, ranging in age from fifteen to nineteen, were also quite confident of their own ability to nurture friendships. They said they see very clearly that a person can become so focused on online communication and texting that he or she loses the ability to communicate in person. Yet all my teenaged interviewees were confident they knew how to handle that challenge. Many of them talked about the priority they place on face-to-face conversations to nurture friendships, in tandem with staying in frequent contact electronically. They said the frequent, brief updates they send and receive through texting and online social networking make it possible to begin face-to-face conversations from a point of connection. They already know the details of their friends' lives, so they can dive into deeper topics when they speak with each other.

Several of the teenagers, however, said they were worried about twelve-year-olds getting cell phones and joining social-networking websites. These older teens worried that younger teens don't have the wisdom to know how to deal with the impersonal nature of electronic communication, which they said is evidenced by the amount of cell-phone and online bullying that goes on among younger teens.

Based on these interviews and on the many articles I've read in recent years about personal relationships in a technological age, just about everyone focuses their concern on other people's use of technology in nurturing friendships. "I know how to cope with it all," they seem to be saying. "But I don't think others do."[3]

Part of my purpose in writing this book is to provide an opportunity to listen to people of all ages talk about friendship. Yes, there are generational differences, particularly in the way relationships are sustained and nurtured. However, I think you'll be amazed at the similarities of commitments and concerns about friendship among people of all ages. I know I was.

This book is an invitation to consider friendship. What makes it work? What are the actions that initiate and nurture friendships? What does it look like to care for friends—to be a friend—in light of the big obstacles to friendship in our time?

QUESTIONS FOR REFLECTION, JOURNALING, DISCUSSION OR ACTION

Each chapter of this book will conclude with a few questions to help you reflect on the ideas in the chapter. Perhaps you'll want to discuss the questions with a friend or family member or in a book group or other small group. Perhaps you'll want to journal about the questions or take some action. Because friendship is such a deeply personal part of our lives, I encourage you to engage personally with the issues I raise in each chapter.

- What is the balance in your life between online, phone and face-to-face communication with friends? What priority do you give to each?

- What do you think and feel about your patterns of connection?

- What role do busyness and distance play in making friendships challenging for you?

- Do you tend to be a technological determinist, believing that technologies greatly influence the kind of communication that can happen when they are used? Or do you tend to adhere to a "technology is neutral" point of view? Are you a technological determinist about some forms of communication, while believing that other technologies are neutral? What are the factors that influence your views on this subject?

- This week, ask two or three people—perhaps friends, colleagues, acquaintances or family members—how they would define *friend* or *friendship*. Think about what you like and don't like about their definitions.

- Spend time praying about the patterns of your friendships. Ask God for insight to illuminate the places for growth in your friendships. Ask God for wisdom to know how to respond.

2

FRIENDSHIP THEN AND NOW

A friend is someone who is there for you and who doesn't gossip about you.
—Sandie, twelve years old

A friend is someone who I respect and someone who gives as well as takes in the relationship. Often friends are people with common interests, values or of similar age, but I have friends who are younger and older where we connect over interests or shared experiences. I rely on my closest friends to tell me the truth I cannot see about myself. But mostly, friends are people who tell me I'm okay and help me think about how to solve the dilemmas of my life. And, of course, friends are people to have fun with.
—Bonnie, an administrator in her sixties

It's my ninth birthday. We're driving through the Midwest, on the move again. This time we're moving from Washington State to Wiesbaden, Germany. I'm excited about Germany. We lived there when I was four years old, and I wonder if I'll recognize anything.

I know what's ahead. I've done this almost every summer that I can remember. We'll arrive a few weeks before school starts, and I'll be bored and lonely during those weeks. I'll play with my five-year-old brother and read a lot. Then school will start, and I'll find a new girlfriend. Maybe two of them. I won't be lonely after I find new friends.

My father is a pilot in the Air Force. I love his stories about the places where he flies. When he gets home from a trip, he gets the map out and shows me where he's been. I accept that having a pilot for a father means that we have to move all the time. But it's hard. It's hard to have a summer birthday and to be on the move each summer. It means I can't invite my friends to a birthday party.

And it's hard leaving my friends every year. But I know how to make new ones. I know how to be friendly, how to take initiative to invite girls over to my house. My mom always helps. She's always glad to help me make connections with new friends.

Mom knows how important friends are. On this cross-country trip, we're stopping to visit grandparents, aunts, uncles and cousins. Plus we're stopping a few times to visit friends of my parents. Mom always keeps up with her friends, and she loves to make new ones. I know what will happen after we arrive in Germany. We'll be living on an American military base, and Mom will be friendly with our new neighbors and the people she meets at church. She'll host parties and dinners for my dad's coworkers and their wives. She'll get to know a bunch of new people, and some of them will become her friends.

And right after Thanksgiving, she'll put away the turkey and stuffing, and clear away the good dishes. She'll get out the old card table and set it up in the living room. She'll spend all her spare time in December sitting at that little table, writing Christmas cards to her friends from all the other places we've lived. She'll write sixty or seventy cards, with a real letter inside each card. She'll tell people how we're doing, in the hopes that they will do the same. She likes to stay connected to friends who don't live near us.

I'm having some weepy moments this summer because of leaving my friends behind, particularly Wendy. She was my closest friend in Washington, and I miss her. But I know it will be okay when we get to Germany. I've always made new friends in every new place. I'll make new friends again. I know how.

WHAT'S AHEAD FOR LYNNE

I can look back on that nine-year-old girl and know what's in store for her. Right after moving into an apartment in Germany, she will meet Becky, a lively girl who lives downstairs. She and Becky will be inseparable for two years, playing Barbie dolls, trading Nancy Drew books and roller skating on their sloping street. Becky will then move to Texas, and Lynne and Becky will exchange letters every month or two for the next ten years.

Becky will write about her fears when her brother has a terrible accident that almost takes his life. She'll write about cute clothes and cute boys. She'll describe her frustration when her mother forbids her to listen to the Beatles because of the casual sexual encounter outlined in the song "Norwegian Wood."

Becky and Lynne will lose touch in their twenties, then reconnect by email in their forties, Becky writing from Florida and Lynne from Seattle. They will stay in touch into their fifties, exchanging pictures and news by email and then on Facebook, using the Internet to bridge a gap of several decades and several thousand miles.

From her many years of exchanging letters with Becky, Lynne will learn the joy of nurturing friendships with people thousands of miles away. She will always be grateful for those moments when a letter from Becky arrived in the mailbox, full of tidbits about daily life.

■ ■ ■

After two years of friendship, Becky will move away from Germany, leaving Lynne feeling a bit empty. But by then Lynne has made some other friends, so she's not too lonely. Besides, Lynne's mom has kept in touch with Wendy's mom, and it turns out Wendy's father is stationed only two hours away in Germany. Wendy and Lynne are able to visit each other on holidays, deepening their friendship that began in second grade in Washington State.

Lynne will move to Virginia the summer she turns twelve. Her family will live in three houses in the next three years, all of them in the same town, but all of them far enough apart that she has to find new friends.

At age twelve, in the seventh grade, Lynne will make friends with a girl in her neighborhood named Terri who loves rock and roll music. They will listen to the radio together. In eighth grade, her closest friend, Susan, is an enthusiastic swimmer, and they will spend hours at the pool. In ninth grade, she'll meet Nancy and Anita, who know some neighborhood boys, an increasingly absorbing topic of interest.

The miracle of the years in Virginia is that Wendy's father has been moved to Washington, D.C., four hours away. Wendy and Lynne are able to continue their holiday visits. Their mothers had to drive them back and forth in Germany, but now the girls are old enough to take the bus on their own. Wendy has become a deep and loving friend, someone who gives Lynne support, admiration and affection.

Lynne will move across the country again at fifteen, after her father's retirement from the Air Force. Her parents will buy a house in Tacoma, Washington, where they will live out the rest of their lives. Lynne will get three years of high school in the same home and at the same school, which feels like a remarkable luxury. Wendy's father will be posted to Anchorage, Alaska, and Lynne will fly to Alaska twice during high school to visit her. As high school students, Wendy and Lynne will exchange dozens of letters, supporting each other through the ups and downs of teenage life.

From Wendy, Lynne will learn the deep joy of being accepted just the way she is. The kind of love that Wendy gives to Lynne will be an anchor for Lynne many times in the midst of teenage angst and self-discovery.

If the nine-year-old Lynne had known that she had another four moves ahead of her before high school, would she have been so willing to engage in new friendships? If she had known she would be able to play with Becky for only two years, and with

Terri, Susan, Anita and Nancy for only one year each, would she have been so willing to build relationships with them?

That nine-year-old would have answered, "Yes!" Because her mother kept up with her friends through letters and visits, that young girl saw clearly that each person we meet has the potential to become a friend for life.

LESSONS LEARNED

What did I learn about friendship from this unusual childhood? That friendship is as essential to me as breathing, that friendship requires a lot of work and that this work is some of the most satisfying we can ever do. That the work of friendship involves a great deal of initiating and requires that we reach beyond ourselves. Over and over.

I also learned that friendship requires forbearance. Each of my childhood friends had such different personalities, and I learned to be interested in and care about what was important to each of them. Without that willingness to engage with the passions of another person's life, I would have been lonely. And I really, truly hated feeling lonely.

The reflection about friendship I've been doing since childhood stands in a long tradition. People have been analyzing and dissecting friendship for millennia. One of the earliest known pieces of literature, *The Epic of Gilgamesh*, records the friendship between Gilgamesh and Enkidu. The most complete version of this epic poem dates from the seventh century before Christ, but scholars believe the story itself is much older than that. In the ancient Greek and Roman worlds, countless stories of friendship were recounted in plays and other forms of literature. In the fourth century before Christ, Aristotle wrote about friendship in the *Nicomachean Ethics*, and in the first century before Christ, Cicero wrote *On Friendship*.

A focus on friendship in many forms of literature has continued until today. Novels and movies present a wide variety of friendships. Some of the most popular TV shows of the recent decades, such as *Seinfeld* and *Friends*, portray groups of friends.

Friendship as a topic of study crosses academic fields. Friendships among animals are studied by biologists; friendships among people in other cultures are studied by anthropologists; and the

> **When to the sessions of sweet silent thought**
>
> **I summon up remembrance of things past,**
>
> **I sigh the lack of many a thing I sought,**
>
> **And with old woes new wail my dear time's waste:**
>
> **Then can I drown an eye, unused to flow,**
>
> **For precious friends hid in death's dateless night,**
>
> **And weep afresh love's long since cancelled woe,**
>
> **And moan the expense of many a vanished sight:**
>
> **Then can I grieve at grievances foregone,**
>
> **And heavily from woe to woe tell o'er**
>
> **The sad account of fore-bemoaned moan,**
>
> **Which I new pay as if not paid before.**
>
> **But if the while I think on thee, dear friend,**
>
> **All losses are restor'd and sorrows end.**
>
> *WILLIAM SHAKESPEARE (c. 1564–1616)*

psychological needs addressed by friends are explored by psychologists. Sociologists study friendship patterns in society, and most religions give assent to the significance of friendship.

However, despite the study of friendship conducted by academics and despite the frequent portrayal of friendships in TV shows, movies and novels, we don't do a lot of reflection about friendship. If you thumb through a stack of men's and women's magazines, you'll find numerous articles about dating, sex, marriage and parent-child relationships, but very little about friendship. The same is true of TV and radio talk shows, sermons and adult education classes in community centers and churches. In recent years, when friendship appears in articles or on talk shows, the focus often centers on the implications of Facebook and other social-networking websites for friendship or the question of whether friendship in our time is endangered. Very little analysis is conducted to help us create, nurture and maintain friendships.

Romantic and family relationships usually take priority in our analysis of human connections, yet for most people friends are a powerful anchor in times of storm and a rich source of companionship, affirmation, acceptance and love. The characteristics of a good friendship have endured throughout the millennia: loyalty, affection, respect, sympathy, empathy and understanding. Friends often share values, interests and experiences. These characteristics are described in ancient and modern treatises on friendship and illustrated in novels, plays, movies and TV shows. You'll hear many of the same friendship themes in the comments I heard in interviews. We don't seem to have trouble identifying the characteristics of a good friendship. The challenge seems to be to create, nurture and maintain such friendships.

IS FRIENDSHIP DECLINING?

In 1995, a Harvard professor of sociology, Robert Putnam, wrote an academic article called "Bowling Alone."[1] In it, he argued that Americans were increasingly isolated from their neighbors, friends and families, and from the broader society. His quintessential illustration was that Americans used to bowl in leagues, but increasingly they were bowling alone.

Because of the attention Putnam received from the article, he continued to amass evidence about isolation in American culture. He published a book in 2001 that has been widely read and cited, also titled *Bowling Alone*.[2] He documented a drop in engagement with dozens of kinds of voluntary associations and clubs in the United States, including churches, parent-teacher associations, social clubs and sports groups. This drop in engagement illustrated increasing isolation, he argued.

A widely cited 2006 study in the academic journal *American Sociological Review* presented further data relevant to friendship.[3] The researchers investigated the question of how many confidants Americans had. *Confidant* was defined as someone with whom they could discuss serious matters. The researchers used some earlier data from 1985 and replicated the study in 2004, finding that the average number of confidants had dropped between 1985 and 2004, and the number of people who said they had no confidants had increased. Americans were depending more frequently on nuclear family members and spouses, rather than friends, for discussing serious matters. The researchers noted the psychological and physiological problems that are correlated with having fewer friendships.

Interestingly, in 2004 people were more likely to have confidants of another race or ethnicity than they were in 1985, and men and women were not significantly different in their patterns of close connections. Also interesting is the note by the researchers that the question they asked had the word *discuss* in it, and they don't know if research participants included online and cell-phone discussion when they considered their answer to the question.

Bowling Alone and academic studies like the one just cited have been mentioned in countless articles in popular magazines and newspapers. Increasing isolation and a dearth of friendship in contemporary life seem to be accepted as the way things are. These concerns, however, are not new. In 1960, C. S. Lewis made the same kind of argument in his book *The Four Loves*:

> To the Ancients, Friendship seemed the happiest and most fully human of all loves; the crown of life and the school of virtue. The modern world, in comparison, ignores it. We admit of course that besides a wife and family a man needs a few "friends." But the very tone of the admission, and the sort of acquaintanceships which those who make it would describe as "friendships," show clearly that what they are

talking about has very little to do with that *Philia* which Aristotle classified among the virtues or that *Amicitia* on which Cicero wrote a book.[4]

It may be true that deep friendships are declining. Or perhaps it is true, as some have argued, that online community is creating a renaissance of friendship in our time. Or maybe social networking and other forms of online connection are a desperate response to the trends toward isolation in Western countries today. Or perhaps the enthusiastic embrace of all these forms of electronic communication isn't so much a desperate response as a simple indicator of the deep truth that people thrive on connections with others and that they will use whatever means are available to build and sustain relationships. I would love to know which of these scenarios is true, but for the purposes of this book I am not concerned with measuring these trends. Instead I want to listen to the voices of people today about what constitutes a good friendship and how to find and nurture friends.

These are the key questions this book will address:

- How can we make friends today?

- How can we sustain and cultivate the friendships we already have?

- How can we use every means available to make the most of our friendships?

- If loyalty, affection, respect, sympathy, empathy and understanding are timeless characteristics of good friendships, how can we grow in expressing those attributes in the friendships we already have?

- And what role does electronic communication play in the answers to these questions?

PART OF THE ANSWER: LOVE

Ask people to define friendship, and their definition will usually take on a reflective, wistful tone as they talk about how deeply they cherish their friends. "Friendship is the reward on the journey," one person told me. "A friend is one of the most precious gifts in life," commented another.

For me, a definition of friendship is closely connected to a definition of love. When I was in my early twenties, I memorized the whole thirteenth chapter of 1 Corinthians, the famous love chapter. That discipline has born much fruit. Sometimes I'll lie awake at night, worrying about a relationship or going back through a conflict in my mind. At some point, as I thrash around, I'll recite 1 Corinthians 13 to myself, analyzing my behavior through the lens of those beautiful words about love. Often I'll see where I went wrong, or I'll see what I need to do the next day.

That description of love from the apostle Paul helps me to define friendship meaningfully. In Colossians 3, Paul shifts his focus from defining love to expressing it. In some ways, 1 Corinthians 13 treats love as a noun, and Colossians 3 treats it as a verb. These two passages have shaped my understanding of how to be a friend more than any other Scriptures. They have informed me, challenged me and guided me as I have tried to love the people around me and as I have tried to nurture friendships. Many parts of this book are an application of these two passages to the question of friendship in our contemporary context. The interplay between the passages lays out a pathway for negotiating the complex questions related to relationships in our time.

The famous love passage from 1 Corinthians has clear parallels to the characteristics of a good friendship that have been described and valued throughout the ages.

> Love is patient; love is kind; love is not envious or boastful or arrogant or rude. It does not insist on its own way; it is not irritable or resentful; it does not rejoice in wrongdoing, but rejoices in the truth. It bears all things, believes all things, hopes all things, endures all things. Love never ends. (1 Corinthians 13:4-8)

The characteristics of friendship that have endured through the ages—loyalty, affection, respect, sympathy, empathy and understanding—are echoed in 1 Corinthians 13. The patience and kindness of real love undergird the kind of sympathy and empathy that makes friendships work. Refraining from envy, boasting and arrogance lays a foundation for the kind of loyalty and affection that has always been valued in friendship. Rudeness and affection are often opposites, so keeping rude words out of our mouths helps us express affection in a more believable way. To feel and convey understanding for another person, we need to let go of our own way, and we need to hold back on being irritable and resentful.

Paul's wisdom in 1 Corinthians about the characteristics of love is timeless and always helpful. The kind of love he describes is the foundation for a deep friendship.

In Colossians 3 we are challenged to organize our lives relationally around particular virtues that are bound up in and completed by love:

> As God's chosen ones, holy and beloved, clothe yourselves with compassion, kindness, humility, meekness, and patience. Bear with one another and, if anyone has a complaint against another, forgive each other; just as the Lord has forgiven you, so you also must forgive. Above all, clothe yourselves with love, which binds everything together in perfect harmony. And let the peace of Christ rule in your hearts, to which indeed you were called in the one body. And be thankful. Let the word of Christ dwell in you richly; teach and admonish one another in all wisdom; and with gratitude in your hearts sing psalms, hymns, and spiritual songs to God. And whatever you do, in word or deed, do everything in the name of the Lord Jesus, giving thanks to God the Father through him. (Colossians 3:12-17)

The compassion, kindness, humility, meekness and patience mentioned in verse 12 relate closely to the characteristics of a good friend mentioned above. Many of the stories of friendships in this book will illustrate what these characteristics look like in practice.

In later chapters in this book, forgiveness, thankfulness and some of the other themes of this passage from Colossians will be explored when I present the skills of friendship that I heard about in my interviews and that I have learned over the years in my own friendships.

The 1 Corinthians 13 and Colossians 3 passages have been foundational for me in nurturing friendships. These words of Paul call me to set aside my own needs and desires long enough to listen deeply to my friends. These words encourage me to try to see my friends for who they are, admire them for their unique gifts and encourage them to be their best selves. These words challenge me to rely on God in my friendships and to pray for my friends. These words affirm that we become what we do; we become more loving as we act in love.

Focusing on these two passages doesn't mean that I don't say anything about my own needs when I talk with friends. I've always got things on my mind, and I share them freely, perhaps too freely. I need a listening ear as much as anyone else. But these words from the Bible encourage me to be sure my friends have equal opportunity to be the one who receives support and encouragement.

We would do well to ponder friendship illuminated by the kind of love described in these two passages. What does that kind of love look like in real life? Before we can engage with that question, we must first consider how our experiences of love and friendship are changing in the wake of all the technological and cultural changes going on in our time.

QUESTIONS FOR REFLECTION, JOURNALING, DISCUSSION OR ACTION

- What do you believe are the most important characteristics of a friend?

- Who are the people who taught you how to be a friend? What did you learn from them? What aspects of what you learned from them have served you well? Which aspects have not been helpful?

- Are your own friendships growing or dwindling, or a combination of both? What are the factors that influence the health of your friendships? What are the major challenges facing you as you try to be a good friend to the people you already know?

- What writings—parts of the Bible or other books—have influenced you the most regarding relationships, what you give to others and what you expect from others? What have you learned?

- This week, express your thanks in some form—in a conversation, a card, an email—to a person who has taught you something significant about friendship or who modeled friendship to you in a way that was helpful.

- Spend time praying about the role of friendship in your childhood and early life. Ask God for the ability to discern the unconscious patterns that you learned, and ask for wisdom to know how to respond.

3

FRIENDSHIP GOES VIRTUAL

*A friend is someone who will make themselves available
to you when you need help.*
—Christi, an office worker in her thirties

*There are different levels of friendship: walking buddies, email buddies,
neighbors into whose houses you can go and get something out of the
fridge, even when they're not home. The closest friends are the ones who
have seen you behaving badly, and stick it out with you.*
—Anne, a car sales executive in her fifties

On our third Thanksgiving in New Zealand, my husband and I
invited over a group of people who, like us, had no family members nearby. At one point after the meal, I was sitting with two
young married couples in the living room. Three of the four of
them lived thousands of miles from their families, as we did.

I told the two couples that I had received an email that week
from an acquaintance who had said strong words: "Electronic
media encourages isolation and limits personal interaction to a
machine."

"How would you respond to this statement?" I asked.

Marcus, a graduate student in his twenties, answered by telling
us about a friend he'd made on Facebook. "It's a person on the
other end. It might be a machine that's enabling you to be in contact with that person, but it's a person. He's having trouble in his

marriage, and struggles with his job, and my heart goes out to him. I feel concern about him. I pray for him. He has needs and struggles, just like I do."

Marcus was talking about a man he had never met. They became Facebook friends because they both had connections to a church in the city where Marcus grew up. They began a tentative, casual exchange using Facebook's chat feature. The more they communicated with each other, the more Marcus felt he had in common with the other man. "We write back and forth about how to make our marriages better. We talk about struggles with our jobs. He's shared a lot of his fears about his grandmother's declining health and her beliefs in God. It's been a rich relationship for me, even though I've never talked to him face-to-face."

Lia, a music teacher, chimed in. Facebook and email help her keep in touch with friends from home who are now far away. She has never developed an online friendship with someone she doesn't know face-to-face. She views electronic media as a wonderful way to maintain relationships between her annual trips home.

I then asked the two couples a question I've had for a long time. I have two friends who almost never answer emails I send them. But they post regularly on Facebook. On the one hand, I'm delighted they post so often on Facebook, because I love to keep up with their lives. On the other hand, I wish they would answer my emails. I asked if anyone could help me understand what was going on with this pattern.

Amber, a clerk in a jewelry store, said that she sometimes finds email intimidating. The space to write an email is so open-ended, and she feels pressured to write something long and significant. "Besides," she added, "I feel like I need to use good grammar and spend some time making sure everything reads well. When I post something on Facebook about what I'm doing, I can be casual and informal. Grammar doesn't matter as much, and I can do it in a minute or two."

Amber went on to describe the strong sense of connection she has with her friends thousands of miles away because of Facebook. She loves to see the photos her friends post, and she gets a kick out of hearing about the seemingly trivial aspects of their daily lives. Those updates about details—what they ate, what they did after work, what they're reading or thinking about—provide a mosaic of their day-to-day lives so she doesn't feel quite so far away.

Of the four twenty-somethings sitting in my living room at Thanksgiving, Jacob was the only one who still lives within easy driving distance of the place where he grew up. I asked him about the ways he connects with friends, given the fact that so many of his friends are local. To my surprise, he replied that most of his closest friends have moved at least some distance away, some of them to other cities and some of them overseas. He uses email, Skype, Facebook and texting to stay in touch with those distant friends. He uses electronic communication to keep in touch with his friends just as much as Marcus, Lia and Amber do.

All four of the young adults sitting in my living room on that Thanksgiving day agreed that one of the most helpful aspects of Facebook is the fact that they can log on any time to catch up with their friends. It's not like making a phone call, where the other person has to be free at the same time.

CONNECTING AND RECONNECTING

Facebook, more than any computer application that came before it, has enabled old friends, acquaintances and family members to connect with each other. Spencer, in his forties, served in Europe with Youth With a Mission when he was in his early twenties. Those who served together have reconnected with each other on Facebook.

Spencer was stunned to find out that some marriages didn't make it. The children he remembers holding on his lap twenty-some years ago are now adults, with careers and families of their own. At first, reconnecting felt shocking and uncomfortable, because so much had changed for so many people. But after those initial disconcerting months of getting reconnected, he's finding that some of the folks who were soul mates back then are still people with whom he enjoys talking. They share prayer requests and current ministry challenges, sometimes through Facebook, sometimes through email or on Skype.

Will, in his thirties, reconnected with a high-school girlfriend on Facebook, and they ended up getting married. Kitty, an editor in her forties, has reconnected with a group of high-school friends on Facebook. They found each other when one of their classmates died in Iraq. What began as a mournful tribute to a tragic event morphed into discussions of memories and sharing about their lives today. Kitty lives in Washington State, their high school was in Nebraska, and the person who got the ball rolling to establish connections lives in New Mexico, an excellent illustration of the mobility that is so common in our time, which makes online connections so valuable.

Rachel believes Facebook gave her back a sister. Rachel's older sister, Teresa, married quite young and moved overseas with her husband. In the two decades that followed, Rachel and Teresa saw each other rarely and felt they had little in common. Rachel and Teresa were both around forty when they reconnected on Facebook. Seeing the photos each one had posted helped them engage with each other's daily lives, and they began to use the chat option to talk about what they were thinking and feeling. The reconnection they have experienced has been salve to a wound that Rachel felt for more than half her life.

When people use the words *faux* or *imitation* to describe relationships with a strong online component, I usually feel a flush of anger. Some of that anger comes from the wonderful stories people have told me, like the ones I've just described for you. So many people are doing their very best to be faithful to their friends and family members, using every possible means to stay connected and express love.

Some of my anger comes from feeling that my own patterns of friendship are called into question by those words. I spent most of

Sharing Thoughts by Writing

Bella, a financial adviser in her thirties, noted, "I find it easier to share my thoughts by writing them down." She loves email because it enables her to stay in touch with friends all over the world and because it gives her the ability to reflect on her life as she writes.

Other people expressed to me their comfort with various forms of online writing as a way of "talking" with their friends about what they value and what's happening in their lives. This has parallels with recent research about online education, which shows that a combination of online and face-to-face teaching has better outcomes than face-to-face teaching alone, and online education with no face-to-face component has outcomes at least as good as a traditional classroom. Perhaps many students, like Bella, find it easier to "talk" about what they're learning as they write rather than trying to speak up in a classroom setting.

People who are skeptical about relationships that are nurtured online need to listen to people like Bella who find they are more vulnerable and open when they write their thoughts and feelings than when they speak about them. Choosing to be vulnerable in friendships, choosing to share the things we are thinking and feeling, builds intimacy.

my adult life in Seattle, and I have lots of close friends there. But I now live thousands of miles away. Email and Facebook are a lifeline for me, and I strongly resist the notion that my friendships have become faux or imitation just because I can seldom see some of the people I love. Even before I left Seattle, I had several close friends who had moved away, and I kept in touch with them mostly by email. They are valued and precious friends, and our email contact nurtured our closeness. Nothing about the friendships I have continued over time using electronic means of communication feels "pseudo" or "faux."

Some of my anger comes from my childhood experience of moving so often. I learned early that even when a friend lives far away, the friendship can still be meaningful. I remember all the letters Becky and Wendy sent to me when I was a teenager. Those letters felt like an earlier version of the same kind of lifeline I experience today through email and Facebook. I also remember the hundreds and thousands of emails I have sent to friends since email came on the scene about fifteen years ago, writing down the events of my life and my thoughts and feelings, and asking for prayer. Some of those emails were sent to friends who lived close by. Email was handy for communicating with them because our busy schedules sometimes made face-to-face conversations hard to achieve.

In this chapter, I want to make the case that electronic communication, when used wisely, can nurture real relationships. Yes, problems and challenges can be deeply troubling, and the next chapter will present some of those painful and sobering issues. For now, I want to begin to explore the realities of friendship today in a world where electronic communication is embedded in the daily life of many people.

SHARED INTERESTS

The stories above illustrate that email, social networking (such as Facebook) and online video conferencing (such as Skype) help maintain existing friendships and sometimes help nurture new ones. The online world also provides many opportunities for connections between people with similar interests. Often these shared interests grow into friendships.

At eighteen, Sam navigates multiple means of communication nimbly and wisely. He believes the variety of ways of communicating that are now available helped him make friends when he moved to a new city at age fifteen. In his last year of high school, Sam teaches break dancing and competes internationally. He lives in a town of 100,000, and no one else in his town dances at his level. He has found significant connections on a national break-dancing forum website. When he competes in another city, he is able to use the forum to ask if anyone has a place he can stay, and he has met up with wonderful people when he travels because of making contact with them online first.

The break-dancing website keeps him up to date about competitions and events, and he learns about the big names in break dancing and what they're doing. Sam got connected with one of those big names through a variety of online means. He found the man on Facebook and noticed he had an address for instant messaging using MSN. Sam added the man's MSN address to his own computer. Before one of Sam's competitions, he found the courage to send an instant message to ask advice. The famous dancer replied, and Sam views their continued connection through instant messaging "a real honor."

Sam believes that face-to-face interactions usually do the most to build relationships. He met another well-known break-dancer at a competition, and that face-to-face meeting made Sam feel comfortable about contacting him online.

For maintaining relationships between close friends or family members who are far away, Sam likes emails and paper letters better than cell-phone text messages or Facebook updates because "they're thought about and longer. It takes more effort." But he would find it odd if one of his more distant Facebook friends were to send him a paper letter. It would feel "stalker-ish."

Another illustration of the significance of online connections based on shared interests comes from John, a medical doctor in his late forties. Several years ago an unexpected and rare disease rendered John deaf. He had always been an enthusiastic amateur photographer, and the descent into silence rendered photography even more attractive. He has continued to work, and photography has filled much of his time outside of work.

John posts his photos on Flickr, a photo-sharing website. He has developed a cadre of friends around the world who comment on his photos and post photos of their own. On a recent trip to Europe, John and his wife looked up several of the friends he had made on Flickr, cementing the online relationships with in-person meetings.

Simon is another person who has met people with shared interests online. In his case, it's the online gaming community. Online games are increasingly common. Some are played online on websites, and some are played using software that is downloaded into home computers and can be connected online to others playing the game at the same time. Consoles for video games, such as Xbox, can be directly connected to the Internet, and the people who play those games can use headsets to talk to other people playing the game at the same time.

Simon, sixteen, dislikes online social networking and texting. He finds them impersonal because he can't hear the person's tone of voice. However, he greatly enjoys playing games on his Xbox connected to the Internet in which he uses a headset to hear voices of the other players. Simon described the process: "You can create talking parties and connect with the people you know who are playing at the same time. Sometimes my mates from school and I will set up a time to play, and we'll talk to each other as we play. Other times I'll play with people I've met through the gaming community who live in other parts of the country or other parts of the world. I know some of those people pretty well because we play together a lot." Simon likes to hear the voices of his friends as he plays, and he experiences a strong sense of comradeship with the people he games with.

A final example of people with shared interests who develop friendships through online connections comes from Anna, in her forties, who is studying counseling in a distance-learning program. She attends classes twice a year for a week, traveling to another part of the country and meeting with students who come from all over. The bulk of their discussion about what they're learning in each class takes place in online forums set up by their instructors.

The online discussion has been rich, deep and personal. Anna feels very close to the other students, and a web of friendship has developed among them. She is glad she gets to see them twice a year, but much of their connection takes place online. Anna says that her instructors have been surprised by the depth of online conversation. When the instructors set up the online discussion forum, they hoped the students would engage in some depth with the course material, but they had not expected that students would write so personally and so deeply.

NURTURING NEARBY FRIENDSHIPS

What about local, nearby friendships? Why would people choose to use cell-phone texting, email or social networking to communicate with someone they see every day?

Most people would agree that emailing or texting works well for communicating facts and information. "The movie starts at 7:30 not 7:00." "Can't bike Saturday. Sunday instead?" Emailing and texting also work well for communicating information to a group of people; individual phone calls would take much more time.

In addition to relaying information, electronic forms of communication do a great job when sharing photos with people nearby as well as far away. Online sharing of photos and sending photos by cell phone have revolutionized the way most people handle their photos. A high-school youth group goes on a mission trip to Africa, or a work colleague takes a vacation in Asia. Before the trip is completed, photos from Africa or Asia appear on social-networking and photo-sharing websites, on blogs, in email in-boxes and on cell phones. People back home can enjoy the photos and experience a bit of the trip with the travelers.

The same is true of local events. Robert has a thirtieth birthday party, and the photos from his party appear online, to the delight of his friends who attended the party, the friends who couldn't attend and perhaps also the people who weren't invited to the party but wish Robert well as he enters a new decade. Photos of births, baptisms, bar mitzvahs, graduations, weddings and even funerals are shared online. People of all ages are enjoying this aspect of the digital revolution. Friendships are nurtured through the sharing of events through photos, whether those friends and events are local or far away.

Another valuable aspect of online communication for nurturing local friendships is the ability to post or send links to online resources. A friend at work sees a YouTube clip that makes him laugh, so he sends an email with a link to the clip. A friend from church reads an article online about a local ministry, and she posts a link to the article on her Facebook site. A colleague from across town reads a blog post by another colleague and adds a link to the blog on a Twitter post.

I don't have a lot of time to cruise around online, looking for

Understanding Colleagues

Hector, a consultant in his sixties, has found blogs and Facebook to be helpful in getting to know his work colleagues. About a year ago, a new colleague arrived, a serious man with narrowly focused interests, quite difficult for Hector to talk with. Hector has found that this man's blog "humanizes him. There's a safety about reading his thoughts on his blog. I don't have to make conversation with him right then; I can just learn more about him." Over time, Hector has found that reading this colleague's blog has helped him find topics for satisfying conversations.

Another colleague is a very intense, driven person. "I can handle her only in small doses," Hector reported. He finds that her Facebook updates help him stay in touch with what she's doing and thinking, again enabling him to have more focused and satisfying conversations with her when they do talk in person.

These online forms of communication, which are often viewed as impersonal, particularly for people who work in close proximity to each other, have helped Hector accept and understand his colleagues. They have also helped him communicate with them more comfortably in face-to-face settings.

interesting articles and video clips, but I enjoy good articles and video clips a lot. I'm grateful to my online friends, both near and far away, for alerting me to interesting—and funny—things to read about and watch.

With respect to local friendships, not many people would disagree that electronic communication is handy for communicating details, viewing photos and sending links. These are significant components of friendship that should not be underestimated. Certainly all of them can be trivial and superficial, but as a part of an ongoing relationship all of them can communicate love in various forms.

But why would someone use electronic communication to share feelings or bits of news with people who live nearby? Wouldn't it make more sense to have a phone or face-to-face conversation?

SOME HELPFUL CONCEPTS

As we consider how to think about and respond to these changes in communication patterns and as we face the challenges of busyness and mobility for friendship today, two sets of concepts shed light on the issues involved.

Asynchronous versus synchronous. When I became an enthusiastic emailer in the mid-1990s, I found that one of the things I liked about email was that I could write messages when I had time, and those messages would be there waiting for my friends or colleagues to read and answer when they had time. Email is a form of asynchronous online communication; the people participating in that form of communication can do it at different times. Email is instant, like a phone call, yet it does not require that the person be on the other end at the same time.

Part of the popularity of online bulletin boards, online groups and special-interest websites is the fact that they provide a way to connect with people on your own time, in an asynchronous fashion. The woman who has a child with leukemia and the man with a passion for Harley-Davidsons can log onto an online group late at night or on their lunch break. They can read other people's posts and add their own. They don't have to go to a meeting at a set time to make contact with people who share the same interests. Instant messaging, in contrast, is a synchronous form of online communication. Both parties need to be online at the same time. Skype is also a form of synchronous communication. It resembles phone calls, except that it is conducted over the Internet and can involve video as well as audio.

The genius of social-networking websites such as Facebook is that they provide options for both asynchronous and synchronous communication. Participants can post comments and photos and send emails that can be viewed by others on their own time. Social-networking sites also provide the opportunity to "chat," to exchange instant messages with others who are online at the same time. Soon social-networking websites will undoubtedly include options similar to Skype that will enable talking and seeing each other on the screen.

The numerous games people can play on social-networking websites also illustrate the benefits of having synchronous and asynchronous options. People can engage in games with other people even if those other people are not online at the same time. If they happen to be online at the same time, the game can go faster or be accompanied by online chat.

In the same way, the appeal of texting with cell phones comes from the option for both synchronous and asynchronous communication. When people send text messages, the recipients can reply right away if they are free, but if they're busy, the message is waiting there until they have time.

Telephone voicemail messages are a form of asynchronous communication, but listening takes so much more time than reading. Speed of processing makes written messages on a cell phone or computer attractive. The quick pace of exchanging written messages, coupled with the option of doing it either synchronously or asynchronously, gives great flexibility.

Interpersonal Communication:
Asynchronous Versus Synchronous

Asynchronous	Synchronous
letters, written notes and memos	face-to-face conversations
telegraph messages	telephone or cell-phone conversations
voicemail messages	
email	video conferencing
online forums, groups, discussion boards	instant messaging
	Skype
Facebook status updates, comments, email	Facebook chat
Twitter posts	
blog posts and responses	

Texting with a cell phone can be synchronous or asynchronous

Several of the teenagers I interviewed stressed the importance for them of staying in constant touch with their friends when they aren't together, through text messages and Facebook chat. Many of the people in their twenties and thirties I interviewed keep Facebook open on their computers while they work; when they take a break, they check to see what their friends are up to. The options for both synchronous and asynchronous communication make these forms of communication very attractive for busy people. The hectic pace of life is one of the biggest friendship challenges of our time, and the synchronous/asynchronous components of electronic communication, which often require only brief moments to process, make clear why so many people use them to nurture nearby friendships as well as friendships with people far away.

Physically close versus physically distant. Many of the stories in this chapter have stressed the gift of electronic communication for nurturing relationships with people who live far away. In an age of great mobility, with family members and friends in distant states or on distant continents, the new ways to communicate are a wonderful gift.

Most people still give priority to seeing their friends in person. In most cases, for most people, electronic means of communication sustain and nurture relationships until the pleasure of a face-to-face visit is possible. Text messages, emails, instant messages, Skype and social networking can, with intentionality and care, be used to convey love and affection, and they can provide the opportunity for genuine sharing of emotions and concerns. Therefore, these means of communication can do much more than put relationships in a holding pattern until a visit happens. Like letters in years past, they can actually build relationships and nurture intimacy.

But visits are still attractive. As one of my friends pointed out recently, online communication at most engages only one or two of the five senses. Nothing replaces a hug, that wonderful opportunity to touch—and smell—friends while verbally greeting them, hearing their voice and getting a good look at them.

Many of the people I interviewed have spent time reflecting on the balance in their life between relationships with people nearby and relationships with people far away. This kind of reflection will become increasingly necessary with continued growth in mobility. How much time should I spend on friendships with people who are far away, and how much time should I spend developing and nurturing friendships here in this place? As mobility continues to create friendship challenges, each person needs to pray and reflect on that question. (In the next chapter, you'll hear about people who have chosen to limit electronic communication in order to focus more intentionally on people close by.)

And with so many options to communicate electronically with friends who live nearby, reflection will be necessary about the balance of face-to-face communication and electronic communication with those nearby friends. With our busy schedules and large networks of friends, it is not realistic to assert that most communication with nearby friends should be face-to-face. Each pair or group of nearby friends has to find a balance point between electronic communication and face-to-face contact that works for the friendship.

SOCIAL SKILLS STILL MATTER

Several of my teenaged interviewees made a noteworthy observation about social skills, another relevant topic when discussing electronic communication. They noted that the people who are the most socially engaged and popular at school are also popular online. Online social networking requires many of the same skills required in face-to-face relationships: compassion, warmth, kindness, encouragement, engagement, willingness to initiate and ability to listen. Making new friends and nurturing existing friendships require skills that are relevant online and offline, that can be learned and that are significant topics when discussing friendships. (The second half of this book is devoted to an exploration of those skills.)

Making blanket critical statements about the technology used to communicate today is pretty easy to do, while discussing ways to reflect love and compassion with various new forms of communication requires more creativity. The latter is urgently needed today.

A common stereotype from two or three decades ago, the socially inept person who spends hours in front of a computer connecting with people online, no longer seems to match reality. Three decades ago, most of the people who understood computers were techies, people who ate and slept and breathed computers. Perhaps some of them, or most of them, were relationally challenged because of their obsession with technology. Now that cell phones, computers and handheld electronic devices are embedded in everyday life, most people make a fairly seamless transition between various forms of communication, and most of the same kinds of relational challenges apply online and offline.

Still, there are real problems and challenges associated with electronic communication. We will look at them in the next chapter. And there are many other challenges for friendships today that have nothing to do with the virtual world. They result from the complexities of everyday life and the limitations and fears associated with being human. We will consider those challenges in chapter five.

As we consider some of these problems and challenges, I want to encourage an attitude of self-examination and reflection. It is no accident that many of the negative articles about Facebook and Twitter are written by people who don't use them. The finger-pointing I've observed with respect to new communication technologies is a form of looking at the speck in someone else's eye while ignoring the log in our own (see Matthew 7:3-5). I greatly admire the careful choices some people have made to use, limit or avoid many different forms of communication in order to nurture their friendships. May they be a model to all of us, encouraging us to examine our own patterns of relating to people we care about.

QUESTIONS FOR REFLECTION, JOURNALING, DISCUSSION OR ACTION

- List the forms of electronic communication you use. List the pros and cons of each form. Note any concerns you have about the way you use any of them.

- Think about the people you love who are physically distant from you, and note the forms of communication you use to keep in touch with them. Think about the people you love who are physically close to you, and note the forms of communication you use with them. Compare and contrast the forms of communication you use with the two groups of friends, and consider any changes you'd like to make.

- This week, ask two or three more people—friends, colleagues, acquaintances or family members—how they would define *friend* or *friendship*. Ponder the role of electronic communication in maintaining the kind of friendships described by the people you asked.

- What concerns do you have about younger people you know and the way they communicate with their friends? Make a point in the next week or two to have a conversation with someone younger than you about the way they nurture friendships. In the conversation, ask questions and listen. Listen for the ways the younger person talks about the roles of compassion, warmth, kindness, encouragement, engagement and listening in his or her friendships.

- Spend time praying about your current patterns of friendship. Ask God for perception to discern the patterns and habits that shape your current friendships. Ask for the wisdom to know how to respond.

4

CHALLENGES FROM TECHNOLOGY

I think there is a huge confusion between friend and acquaintance. A friend is someone with whom I have a close and deep relationship, someone I can be myself with and who accepts me as I am, even when we have sharp disagreements. Acquaintances are people we know, but with whom the relationship is not deep. By those definitions, most people have few true friends but many acquaintances.
—Bradley, a minister in his fifties

I'll be there for you.
—Theme song from the TV show *Friends*

"Facebook is evil." Steven, a man in his early thirties who recently left his corporate job to become a full-time university student, got our attention when he said those words at a gathering in our home.

He went on to clarify. "Maybe it's more accurate to say that, for me, Facebook was evil. With my addictive personality, I found myself trying to get more and more friends. I couldn't stay away from it for more than a few hours. I had to check it all the time. It took up so much time and emotional energy, and I knew I could have been giving that energy to friends here. Finally I just canceled it all, and now I've got so much more time for other things."

A recent *Zits* comic presented the same idea. Jeremy, the teenager in the strip, tells his mother that he has a huge school project to finish, so he needs her help. She asks if he needs her to research or edit something. Jeremy says no, it's something much more important than that. He brings his laptop computer to her and says, "Change my Facebook password so I don't get sucked into it tonight."

I heard comments about the temptation to spend too much time with electronic forms of communication from people of all ages. When I joined Facebook, someone I knew from Seattle who was one of my new Facebook friends sent me a message: "Welcome to the time suck known as Facebook." Mae, fifteen, noted that Facebook is "a massive time waster. I've spent hours there, looking at people's photos, chatting with several friends at the same time."

The temptations of getting sucked into electronic communication are not limited to social networking, nor are they limited to people in a certain age group. Mildred, in her seventies, got her first cell phone a year ago. She learned how to send text messages, and she loved the instant connection with her many siblings and with her friends. She found herself checking her cell phone every few minutes to see if a text message had arrived. "I finally had to put the cell phone in a drawer in my sideboard so I wouldn't check it all the time. I still keep it there, and I get it out only when I hear the ring that alerts me that a message has arrived or if I need to send one."

ADDICTION

Owen, a twenty-year-old university student, recently made a decision to disengage from an online gaming community. He had gotten increasingly immersed in a particular online game. The more he played, the more he got to know the other people around the world who played it. After a few months of intense gaming, he became involved in the globe-spanning leadership structure of the game. He enjoyed the cognitive challenge of this particular game as well as a sense of connection with people from different countries.

On a typical evening, Owen would say to himself, "I'm going to go online to see how everyone is. Just for fifteen minutes." Three hours later he would look up and realize he hadn't been aware of the time passing.

When his grades came in from his mid-semester assignments, he began to suspect the game was getting in the way of his studies. The more he looked at the pattern of his involvement with the game, the more he realized it was interfering with his local friendships as well. He was simply spending less time hanging out with friends. And he noticed that when friends would walk into his dorm room, he would minimize the game on the computer screen so they wouldn't know what he had been doing.

"Anything can become an addiction," Owen reflected. "Work, for example. Is an online hold a similar kind of addiction? I finally realized there are better things to invest our time in." As he pondered whether or not to quit playing the game, he found himself thinking, *I've got to keep playing; these guys value me!* He had to argue with himself in order to stop. The argument that finally convinced him was the realization he was spending more time than he wanted with people he had never met in person, while spending less time than he wanted with people he knew very well and valued highly. The weakness of purely online relationships, he realized, is that all too often "it's conversation without a context."

Owen made a decision to stop playing entirely, and he thought carefully about how to get closure in the relationships he had developed in the gaming community. He decided he didn't want to simply disappear from the online community, so he announced he was going to leave at the end of the week. He then kept playing for those remaining days.

A few weeks after Owen quit playing, he came across an article that highlighted some warning signs about addiction to technology. He remembers some of the questions because they were relevant to him:

- Is technology getting in the way of relationships?
- Are you spending more time online than you intended?

- Is technology interfering with your school or work performance?

- Are friends or family members complaining about the amount of time and energy you spend online?

- Are you frequently choosing to spend time online rather than with family and friends?

Owen realized that if he had gone through this list during the months he was playing the game so intensely and if he had been willing to be honest in answering the questions, he would have answered yes to all of them.

Several of the questions on the list related to feeling depressed, moody, restless or nervous either online or offline. Owen couldn't relate to those questions at all. He believes he caught his addiction before it advanced very far.

In the six months after Owen quit playing the game that had occupied so much of his time, he logged on a handful of times to

Fasting from Technology

People of all ages, but particularly younger people, are increasingly experimenting with technology fasts. They put away their cell phone, computer, iPod and other electronic devices for a specific period, perhaps a day or a weekend.

Fasting from technology helps to bring a lot of things into perspective. A technology fast can provide the opportunity to rediscover the joys of a relaxed meal with a friend or a leisurely conversation while taking a walk or washing the car together. A technology fast can expose relational patterns such as imbalances between electronic and face-to-face communication or between time spent with distant friends and friends who live nearby.

Fasting from technology can also free up time for prayer. One topic of prayer might be to ask for God's guidance about wise use of technology.

check the rankings of his friends. He never played that game again after he quit. "I've been tempted," he said. Owen still plays other online games, but only with face-to-face friends. They log on at the same time and compete with each other. He sees that kind of gaming as a part of a wider relationship he has with those friends.

Those who use any form of communication technology should examine themselves from time to time to see if any addictive behaviors are developing. It can happen to anyone, any time.

COMMUNICATING WITH FRIENDS IN AGES PAST

A brief survey of how we got here will help bring clarity to this discussion of friendship patterns today. Let's pause to imagine the ways friends might have communicated with each other a thousand years ago.

Most conversation between friends a thousand years ago would have been verbal, either face-to-face or by passing along a verbal message to be delivered by someone else. On rare occasions, friends might have sent a written message, perhaps a letter or a short note. The written message would have been delivered by someone who walked, took a boat or traveled on horseback or in a horse-drawn carriage.

Because few people were literate, the written message might have been dictated to someone who knew how to read and write, and that message might have been read aloud on the other end by the village priest or another educated person. Because of limited transportation and literacy, written messages would have been unusual.

Communication between friends a thousand years ago wasn't much different than it had been a thousand or two thousand years before that. Without widespread literacy, most communication between friends was oral, either face-to-face or through an oral message passed on by a messenger.

The invention of the printing press in the fifteenth century changed mass communication and contributed to increased literacy. Paper got cheaper as well, so letter writing between friends became a bit more common. However, getting letters to another person remained difficult until inexpensive postal systems came on the scene, mostly in the nineteenth or twentieth centuries.

The telegraph, increasingly common in the second half of the 1800s, made a slight change in the options for communication between friends. It was a quick way to send news, but it was expensive, so telegraph messages between family members or friends were usually reserved for emergencies. And before travel became common, most friends lived in close proximity to each other. Before 1900, most friends probably lived their entire lives without sending a telegraph message—or a letter—to each other.[1]

The ways friends communicated with each other didn't change very much until after 1900. Letter writing increased a great deal in the twentieth century, and supported and nurtured many friendships, so perhaps it could be viewed as the first real shift in options for communication between friends. However, the telephone was the first invention to make a major change in the way friends interacted on a daily basis. Because telephones have been common in homes for the better part of a century, very few people remember life without them. Many older adults remember party lines, when phone calls were not private. They also remember when long-distance phone calls were so expensive they were used much like the telegraph, only to shout "hello" on holidays and to briefly convey very good or very bad news.

What most people don't realize is that when telephones began to be installed in homes, concerns were raised by social and religious leaders. Telephones, some experts asserted, might damage relationships. Because the nonverbal cues that enrich and inform relationships are lost when people talk on the phone, commentators thought this could create fundamental and damaging changes in interpersonal communication. Phone calls out of the blue would interrupt the tasks of daily life and cause increased anxiety.

Claude Fischer, in his fascinating history of the telephone titled *America Calling*, notes that in the early decades of the twentieth century, some observers worried that the telephone encouraged "too much familiarity and incivility" and that it also tended to undermine solidarity in neighborhoods.[2] Fischer cites the example of a 1926 Roman Catholic adult education committee in the Archdiocese of San Francisco that proposed a topic for group discussion: "Do modern inventions help or mar character and health?" One of the specific questions proposed for discussion was "Does the telephone break up home life and the old practice of visiting friends?"[3]

Some people may feel that telephones have compromised friendships and increased anxiety, but many people would assert that telephones have nurtured relationships and calmed fears. A quick phone call to give assurance of safe arrival after a long trip. A call to express concern and compassion after a death in the family. A call to check on a sick friend. A call to talk over a painful conflict at work. A call to debrief with a friend after an argument with a teenaged child.

Over the last century, phone calls became cheaper and more private, but communication between friends didn't really change again until the 1990s, when cell phones, email and the Internet became common. The big communication advances of the early and mid-twentieth century—radio, movies and television—involved mass communication, not communication between friends.

Email appeared on the scene in the 1970s and 1980s in academic circles and in the 1990s for most of the rest of us. Online discussion groups, instant messaging and inexpensive cell phones became increasingly common in the 1990s, but many of the other communication technologies that are currently shaping friendships didn't appear until the twenty-first century or weren't commonly used until then: digital cameras, cameras in cell phones, cell-phone texting, blogs, Skype and social-networking websites. These are all remarkably new. No wonder we need to engage in careful and creative thinking in order to use them wisely.

The many strong pro and con opinions about online social networking and other forms of electronic communication come in part from the fact that so many new forms of communication have exploded into our world in the past few years. We simply don't know the best ways to use them yet. Whatever our age, we cannot rely on parents or other older people for wisdom. Because of generational patterns in the use of new communication technologies, older people are generally even more baffled than younger people.

The plethora of communications options in our time has brought about an unexpected challenge. Patterns of communication have become highly individualized, a trend that impacts people of all ages, no matter what their convictions about how people should communicate. We have only just begun to deal with the implications of the fact that different people use diverse ways to communicate.

INDIVIDUALIZATION OF COMMUNICATION

Recently I logged on to Facebook, and on my news feed I found a status update from a close friend's husband: "Looking forward to baby #3, apart from the lack of sleep part." I immediately sent an email to my friend, congratulating her on the pregnancy.

She wrote back: "Arghh! I wanted to tell you myself! Well, thank you for not being angry that you found out in such an impersonal way." She said she hadn't known that her husband was going to post the news on Facebook. She went on to say how tired she had been, which was the precise reason I wasn't offended that I had learned the news on Facebook. I figured she was experiencing the fatigue of early pregnancy and hadn't had time to write an email to me.

I also found myself pondering her use of the word *impersonal* to describe a Facebook communication. I know many of the people I've interviewed for this book would not agree that they find Facebook impersonal.

I learned about another pregnancy only a few days later, also through a Facebook post. In this case, the expectant mom is a person I enjoy very much and consider to be a friend, but we are not close friends. We probably have contact with each other only once or twice a year. I found myself wondering, *If I had missed her Facebook post, how long would it have been before I knew about her pregnancy?* We're not close enough friends that I would expect her to email me with the news.

One of the growing challenges in maintaining friendships today is the multiple ways to connect. The many options for communication have resulted in the disconcerting fact that most people choose the one or two ways they are most comfortable with. This means that a message sent to a friend might not be read or listened to if it is sent in a form that the friend doesn't often use.

Simon, sixteen, doesn't like texting on his cell phone, even though

Shifts in Email Use

Some of my older interviewees write long, leisurely emails to friends, similar to the letters friends and family members sent each other throughout most of the 1900s. In contrast, some of my interviewees in their twenties and thirties expressed frustration with email, saying they prefer short emails and sometimes don't bother to read long emails. Only one of my teenaged interviewees uses email to stay in touch with friends; the rest of them use email only for communicating with adults such as teachers or relatives. For communication with friends who are not physically present, they prefer instant messaging, Facebook or texting, all of which involve brief exchanges and are more like casual conversations in which the conversational ball bounces around quickly.

Are teens and young adults losing the ability to talk deeply with others? All the teens and young adults I interviewed insist that they are not losing that skill. They say that the brief exchanges they prefer through instant messaging, social networking and texting keep relationships fresh, alive and up to date so that when they see their friends face-to-face, they can pick up where they left off and talk deeply about significant matters.

all his friends do it. "It's too impersonal," he says. He uses texting for getting and giving information, but never for anything personal.

Clare, eighteen, uses cell-phone texts and Facebook frequently, but seldom checks her email. Ariel, in her late twenties, uses Facebook and email but seldom sends text messages. Andreas, also in his late twenties, relies almost entirely on text messages to communicate. He doesn't listen to oral messages that collect on his cell phone; he simply ignores them. Kirsten, forty, doesn't like Facebook and checks her email only occasionally, but she texts with her friends all the time.

Jared, in his thirties, recently quit Facebook. He calls it a "time waster" that nurtures "pseudocommunity." He finds most Facebook status updates to be banal, and he also has concerns about privacy. Jared reads numerous blogs every day and makes posts on his own blog several times a week. After six years, he still loves the whole process of blogging. He finds other people's blog posts and the comments people make about his own blog posts to be infinitely more interesting than anything he used to read on Facebook. For him, blogging has nurtured a community of people who share ideas and resources.

Those of us who are older find it tempting to believe that people in the younger generations all use the same technologies to communicate with each other. If one teenager or twenty-something uses Facebook or texting, and loves it, we tend to assume all teens do. In contrast to that assumption, my interviews revealed a pattern of individualization of communication at all ages. There are trends for each generation, but a surprising number of exceptions to the trends at all ages.

My younger son, in his late twenties, maintains an extensive network of friendships and uses many ways to stay in touch with his friends. He realizes he will connect with some friends by text message, some by email, some through Facebook, some through instant messaging and yet others through blogging. He is unusual in his commitment to connect with all his friends through whatever means of communication they like best, rather than simply using the forms he prefers. It is no accident my son has good friends all over the world. He keeps in contact with them.

Email is my preferred means of communication, and Facebook is rapidly becoming a close second. Many of my closest friends are not on Facebook or don't use it very much, but some other friends rarely use email and are very active on Facebook. I'm trying to learn to be more like my son, using the form of communication that fits the priorities of the person I want to connect with.

When we moved to New Zealand from Seattle three years ago, one of my Seattle friends asked if I'd be willing to write paper letters to her. She dislikes writing long emails, and she loves the feel of paper. "I like to touch and hold the letter," she said. "It's like a part of you coming through." She's perfectly happy to use email for communicating information, but for communicating thoughts and feelings, she prefers paper letters.

She's a special friend, so I agreed to exchange letters with her. I've enjoyed the process of sitting down with pen and paper every few months to write a long letter. But I can type so much more quickly than I can handwrite, so I occasionally find it frustrating that we correspond this way. But I do it because I value her friendship so much.

When I left Seattle, neither of us was on Facebook. Now, three years later, we are both on Facebook. While I still love her letters, seeing the photos and comments she posts on Facebook contributes to my sense of participation in her life.

INTENTIONALITY IN FRIENDSHIP TODAY

In our time, with so many different options for communication, intentionality in friendship involves making choices to honor the favored communication patterns of the people we care about. It requires intentional effort to avoid those hurtful scenarios when someone we love doesn't receive important news—an engagement, a pregnancy, an illness, a birth or death in the family—because she or he doesn't check Facebook, email or cell-phone voicemail very often.

In our time, intentionality in friendship also involves making choices to try new communication technologies to stay in touch. Kacie, a teacher in her thirties, said, "I tend to resist new ways to communicate. I was the last person in my circle of friends to get a cell phone, and I was one of the last to join Facebook. But there comes the day when you buckle and get the new technology. You're opting out of relationships if you don't get whatever it is that other people are using."

She has observed the way her parents, in their seventies, have navigated these changes.

> I've watched my parents get email, because if you don't, you won't get Christmas letters from your old friends anymore. Hardly anyone sends paper Christmas letters these days; everyone sends them by email. But I'm concerned about my father. My mother has learned how to send text messages and how to use email, so she keeps up the connections both for her and for my father. What will happen if she gets sick or dies before he does?

Kacie is also concerned about the changes in privacy. She finds herself more self-conscious in photos and videos. "I've seen photos posted online of people drunk and doing crazy things at parties," she says. "The photos can be taken with a cell phone, so you don't even know that they're being taken. It makes me feel more on edge when photos are being taken, because I could end up seeing that photo posted online somewhere."

As someone who has struggled with weight and who is very self-conscious about photos that make me look fat, I find it frustrating when friends post photos of me that I view as unflattering. Now that people can post photos so easily online, photos can appear anywhere, anytime, at the discretion of the person who took the photo, not the person who is featured in it.

We've gained the ability to post photos easily and quickly so we can share them with friends, but we've lost a sense of privacy. We've gained the ability to connect in numerous ways, but we've lost consistency in communication. Sometimes it's baffling to figure out how to get a message to a friend in a form she or he will listen to or read. This gaining and losing spills over into many aspects of communication with friends today.

GAINS AND LOSSES

Every new communication technology contributes something positive and takes something else away. Let's go back to the telephone for a moment. The commentators who were negative about the telephone in the early 1900s were concerned about the fact that nonverbal cues were lost and that a phone call could interrupt the tasks of daily life. Was something gained to make up for these losses? Yes, of course. The telephone gave us the ability to have a conversation with someone who was not physically present. Compared to the telegraph, the telephone was cheaper and was available in homes.

In some phone conversations, the absence of the physical presence of the other person turns out to be surprisingly positive. I have vivid memories of long conversations with a high-school boyfriend. On the phone, we were able to talk intimately about our thoughts and feelings in a way that we didn't do when we were in the same place. Part of it came from the removal of the temptation to kiss each other that we felt when we were physically in the same place. But part of it came from the absence of visual cues, so we focused more intently on tone of voice and emotional content.

The telephone took away nonverbal communication and gave back at least two things: the ability to communicate with someone who is not physically present and the opportunity to focus on the other person's voice without being distracted by his or her physical presence. Telephones may have shaped us as communicators, making us more attentive to small changes in tone of voice in the absence of nonverbal cues.

Some of my older interviewees talked about another gift of writing to friends. They described the way they are able to share deep emotions when writing emails or letters. The removal of the distraction of the other person's physical presence enables them to access their own thoughts and feelings, much like earlier generations did when they wrote letters. Several teenagers and people in their twenties said that they are amazed at how deeply some of their friends share their feelings using text messages. They described long, intense conversations with friends, conducted entirely by texting, again reflecting the gift of removing the distraction of the other person's physical presence.

Many people find today's relentless innovation in communication technologies to be intimidating and exhausting. Sure, new technologies provide new opportunities to connect, but right after you master one, another comes along. It feels overwhelming to learn how to use one new form of communication after another.

I've read so many negative articles about Facebook and Twitter, describing how damaging they are, from people who have never used them. I find it hard to take those articles seriously. Perhaps many of these articles originate in a deep frustration with the endless stream of new ways to communicate. Perhaps some of those writers are hoping they can convince themselves that online social networking doesn't nurture real relationships so that they won't have to learn how to use yet one more new technology.

Some of the concern about online social networking comes from people who use it. I pay careful attention to those opinions. One of those comments came from Josh, a video editor in his thirties. Josh has numerous close relationships, and he enjoys keeping up with a wide circle of people through Facebook. He also recognizes that, in his circle of friends, Facebook is essential because many invitations to parties and other events are posted on Facebook and nowhere else.

However, Josh has reservations about Facebook: "With Facebook, my contact with my friends is almost too convenient. I can

control my contact with them too much. They are compartmentalized into those moments when I choose to go online to Facebook."

Another concern about Facebook was expressed by several
people ranging in age from twenty to fifty. They used the word
voyeuristic to describe the way they sometimes feel when they go
on Facebook, as if they are peering into people's lives much like a
window peeper might do. Oddly, I seldom feel that way on Facebook, because I mostly look at the photos and comments posted

---

A Creative Solution

Harriet, in her seventies, kept getting invitations to join Facebook, so she
finally created a Facebook account. However, she logged in rarely, and
each time she did, she felt guilty about the messages she found waiting
for her there. Harriet talked with her daughter, Kacie, about her frustration
with the situation.

Kacie had a creative idea. She wrote a status update for Harriet: "I'm
not ready for Facebook yet. Please contact me by email instead." This has
enabled Harriet's old friends to find her and friend her on Facebook, but it
allows for their expectations of Harriet's level of engagement on
Facebook to be realistic. And it encourages them to send her an email.

---

by people I know, and I enjoy feeling connected to those people.
However, I have felt voyeuristic reading blogs. I sometimes read
blogs written by people I don't know because I'm looking for interesting ideas, but I have no desire to read their intensely personal
comments. On occasion I have stopped reading in the middle of a
blog post, or a response to a blog post, because something inside
me was cringing and saying, "Too much information!"

One woman in her thirties echoed my thoughts. "Facebook is a
two-edged sword. It gives us too much information about everyone
and everything. I don't necessarily want to be getting daily updates
from someone from the past that I don't have a very close connection

with. Yet I find Facebook more manageable than email for keeping in touch with a large number of people, because I can get smaller bits of news about what my friends are doing and vice versa."

DANGERS AND CHALLENGES

Written electronic messages are quick and easy to process, so they give access to other people's thoughts and feelings in a small amount of time. This rapid-fire access to people's thoughts and feelings, as well as photographs of their lives, can help people feel connected to each other. But this access also contributes to the feelings of being voyeurs. The ability to rapidly "consume" people's thoughts, feelings and photographs whenever we feel like it gives relationships with friends consumeristic components. The ability to do this on our own time, in our own space, gives relationships individualistic, compartmentalized, self-focused aspects. All of this can be enticing and even addictive. Truly the new communication technologies are two-edged swords.

Many commentators note that most forms of electronic communication (with the exception of Skype) take away nonverbal communication like the telephone does. In addition, they take away tone of voice. Many of the alarms being sounded about electronic messages relate to this lack of nonverbal and tone-of-voice connection. But letters lack the same features, and no one has expressed a lot of concern about them.

I believe the biggest danger with electronic messages lies in the speed of processing and the sheer amount of information about other people that is available, which can dull our awareness that human relationships are precious, that friends are one of the biggest gifts that life can give. Electronic communication can contribute to relationships becoming individualistic, compartmentalized transactions. If we care about healthy friendships, this danger must be addressed.

Life in Western countries in the twenty-first century is characterized by rampant individualism and consumerism, and online

communication can reinforce it. Engaging in caring and supportive relationships that have a significant online component requires
intentionality. As individuals and as groups of friends, we need to
engage in a lot of creative thinking to address the challenges of
new technologies. We need to apply age-old truths about good
relationships to new ways of connecting with friends.

Melanie and Susan, both twenty, illustrate the individualization of communication, discussed earlier in the chapter, along
with a communal response to the downsides of electronic communication. Melanie approached me at a conference where I had
been speaking about friendship and said, "A lot of my friends are
leaving Facebook. They find it too absorbing. Particularly during
exam time, lots of them quit because they find they don't get
enough studying done. Spending time on Facebook is too tempting and takes them away from other things they value more."

As Melanie finished talking, Susan joined us. Melanie intro-
duced her to me and said, "Susan is one of those friends. She got
sick of Facebook and quit."

My immediate response was curiosity. I asked Susan, "How do
you stay in touch with your friends?" She replied that texting was
her primary way of staying connected.

Many people in their twenties and thirties have told me that
Facebook is essential for receiving invitations and information
about events, so I asked another question: "How do you find out
about parties and events if you're not on Facebook?"

She responded, "I depend on my friends like Melanie, who are
still on Facebook, to let me know. They pay attention to the events
and invitations posted there, and they text me." She looked a bit
sheepish because she was acknowledging the centrality of Facebook for her circle of friends, while also acknowledging her dependence on friends like Melanie to keep her in the loop.

Generational patterns in communication are clearly evident
today, but my conversation with Susan and Melanie demonstrates
that no generation has a monolithic communication style. Indi-

viduals are making diverse and creative choices in the ways they communicate with friends as they experiment with options and as they grow in self-awareness. Some people can log on to a social-networking website, and then log off when they intended to. Their use of social networking feels appropriate and healthy. Others find it too absorbing, even addictive, and it gets in the way of other priorities. Each person has to experiment to find patterns of communication that work in her or his own life and circle of friends.

THE CONTENT AND THE TECHNOLOGIES

I recently heard an interview with Bruce Ramos, lighting director for four U2 concert tours. He said that what made U2 concerts great was the focus on what they had to say, and for each concert he always took a lot of time to ponder that question. After the message was clarified, he could turn his attention to the technology required to communicate the message, which took much less time to figure out. He stressed that content comes first, technology second.

I was struck with the way his words apply to friendship in this age of so many communication technologies. "Content first, technology second" is a relevant concept to keep in mind with respect to specific communications with friends. What matters is what I want to say. Then I need to think about how best to convey that message to my friend. On an even deeper level, "content first, technology second" helps keep the broader focus in the right place. What matters is the friendship itself, the relationship with another person. All forms of communication need to serve friendship, not the other way around.

In fact, the content of friendship is love. Let's look again at the words in 1 Corinthians that describe love. I invite you to read these words one more time, this time keeping in mind the challenges of electronic communication.

Love is patient; love is kind; love is not envious or boastful or arrogant or rude. It does not insist on its own way; it is not irritable or resentful; it does not rejoice in wrongdoing, but rejoices in the truth. It bears all things, believes all things, hopes all things, endures all things. Love never ends. (1 Corinthians 13:4-8)

Love for his friends who were in close proximity motivated Owen to drop online gaming, which connected him with people all over the world. Those people had become friends as well, but Owen believed God was calling him to focus on his nearby friends because those relationships had the potential to be deeper. He felt those relationships with people in close proximity were more likely to reflect the kind of love described in 1 Corinthians 13.

Love motivates my younger son to use communication technologies that are comfortable for his friends, rather than just the ones he prefers. Love helps us avoid posting embarrassing photos of others. The photo of our friend in an awkward pose may be funny, but would it be kind to post it without asking our friend's permission? Love encourages us to slow down when we read posts on a blog or a social-networking website, to engage in the kind of patience and receptivity that allows us to hear what's going on in a friend's life and perhaps pause to pray for them. Love helps us keep our envy under control when a friend accomplishes something wonderful, and love helps us rejoice with them and post words online that are affirming and encouraging. Love keeps us from posting rude, glib or flippant words that can hurt. Using social networking or texting to bully or hurt others is wrong, and the principles of love help us understand why.

The kind of love described in 1 Corinthians 13 provides insight about why it feels uncomfortable to engage in voyeurism online. We know intuitively that we were created for something more than mindless accumulation of details about other people's lives. We know that people are more than objects. When we sense that the online world objectifies others, we feel slimy and yucky.

How can we avoid voyeurism, objectification, bullying and the other negative sides to electronic communication? By placing some

The Challenges of Cell-Phone Texting

Polly has three daughters, fourteen, eighteen and twenty-one. The family has moved several times. The girls use Facebook and texting to nurture friendships both near and far.

Polly reflected on the patterns of relationships she has observed in her girls:

I'm not worried about Facebook. There doesn't seem to be much room for online predators on Facebook, and I don't see my girls or their friends engaging in a lot of negative communication there. They seem to take time to think about what they post. But I am deeply concerned about texting. It's just too easy to send off a quick message when you're irritated, hurt or frustrated.

My daughters have shown me some of the text messages they get from their friends. Sometimes they're so negative. If a girl feels hurt, she can fire off a message right away, criticizing the person who hurt her. Gossip seems to fly around through texting, and some of the gossip borders on bullying. They do things with texting without thinking about it.

Careful communication always matters. Thinking before speaking, good advice through the ages, carries over to the world of electronic communication.

limits on the amount of time spent on electronic communication with friends. By choosing to see friends face-to-face whenever possible. By fasting from technology occasionally to gain perspective and to pray for guidance about using it wisely. By talking with friends about the best ways to nurture relationships. By praying each day that all our relationships, online or offline, would be characterized by love, care and compassion. By asking for God's help to grow in clothing ourselves in love, patience, kindness and compassion.

I long for leaders, ministers, writers and observers of culture to stop describing electronic communication in black-and-white terms, to stop viewing it as all bad or, as occasionally happens, as all good. Almost all relationships these days have electronic components. Electronic communication can be helpful in nurturing relationships across the miles and in the midst of busy schedules. It can also be addictive, impersonal, consumeristic and individualistic. The challenge is to focus on content first and technology second. The content of friendship is love, and we need to grow in showing love by every means available to us.

Because so many forms of connecting with friends are so new, it will take some time for us to find the best ways to use new communication technologies to show love and nurture friendships. It will take creativity and self-discipline to learn to use electronic communication as a means to demonstrate care and compassion, just like it takes creativity and self-discipline to show care and compassion in face-to-face settings.

In the next chapter, we turn to friendship challenges that don't relate to new ways to communicate. Many of these other challenges are precipitated by new trends in everyday life. Whether we like it or not, many aspects of life are changing with unprecedented speed. God's character and love, however, are timeless, and we need our unchanging God as an anchor and guide more than ever.

QUESTIONS FOR REFLECTION, JOURNALING, DISCUSSION OR ACTION

- What are your biggest friendship challenges related to various forms of communication?

- What do you experience to be the blessings and limitations of electronic communication? In what ways do you take advantage of the blessings? How do you compensate for the limitations? Are there ways you could compensate further?

- Have you ever wondered if you were engaging in addictive behaviors related to a particular form of communication? What symptoms have you observed in yourself? How have you handled it? With whom have you or could you talk about it?

- Consider a technology fast. Which technologies might be productive to fast from? How long can you imagine fasting from them? What might you pray for as you fast?

- Have you experienced the challenge of the individualization of communication, with different people you know using different ways of keeping in touch? Have you been stretched in good ways by this phenomenon? In frustrating ways?

- This week, ask a friend or family member for feedback about your friendship patterns. Ask them to tell you what they think you do well in your friendships, and ask if they have any concerns about the way you conduct your friendships.

- Spend time praying about your patterns of using electronic communication in friendships. Ask God to challenge you and guide you.

5

CHALLENGES BEYOND
TECHNOLOGY

*A friend is someone you can count on, someone who will be there for you,
a person who you can be open and honest with. A friend is like a pair of old
slippers; you can put them on and feel comfortable and just be yourself.*
—Juliet, a minister in her thirties

*Nobody sees a flower—really—it is so small—we haven't time—and to see
takes time, like to have a friend takes time.*
—Georgia O'Keeffe (1887–1986)

Some of the challenges of friendship in our time have nothing to do with new ways to communicate. Busyness, distance, unwillingness to reveal weaknesses, and fear of vulnerability can affect anyone. Some friendship challenges relate to specific personalities or choices made by other people. The purpose of this chapter is to open up some of these challenges, validate that they are not uncommon and encourage discussion, reflection and prayer about them.

Some of these challenges won't change very much after discussion, reflection and prayer. Some of them just have to be lived with. At the very least, by openly acknowledging these challenges, people who experience them will know that they are not alone in facing them.

However, bringing them out in the open, discussing them, reflecting on and praying about them may result in some helpful movement or change. During the writing of this book, I saw the resolution of a small friendship challenge. Did that situation change because I was thinking and praying about friendship? Did it change because another friend encouraged me not to give up hope? Whatever the reason, I was watching for signs of change and cautiously praying for them as well, and a difficult situation became somewhat easier. I'm so grateful.

BUSYNESS AND DISTANCE

The two biggest challenges for friendship today that do not relate to technology—busyness and distance—came up in my interviews over and over. Jessica, a nurse in her fifties, reflected on both of them.

Jessica lives in Seattle, and she met her three closest friends there. One by one, her friends moved away. One now lives three hours away, and two of her friends live overseas. She keeps in touch with them through email, phone calls and visits, but it's not the same.

Jessica works three days a week, and she's grateful she doesn't have to work full time. But she has a wide extended family in Seattle, and family involvements take up a lot of her time. She feels continually pressed for time, a pressure that affects her friendships. Jessica reflected on her pattern of friendships,

> When I make a friend, that person is a friend for life. I'm careful. I don't make a lot of new friends, because I already have close friends. But so many of them are so far away.
>
> I long for spontaneous connections with friends. Those kinds of connections seem to be totally lost today because of busyness, stress and age in life. I long to live in a neighborhood where people stop by and have coffee and tea, and chat. I'm a person who likes plans and schedules, but there's a different quality of interaction that happens when it's spontane-

ous. There's a naturalness. There are snippets of conversation that feel more real.

When you plan a dinner or coffee with friends you haven't seen for a while, you have to organize your thoughts. You have to think about everything you want to catch up on and cover it in two or three hours. You would lose friends if you didn't have those planned times together, but something is lost by not having informal contacts, a few minutes here and there, like you have in a neighborhood where people stop by and chat. As children, most of us had a lot of that, and even in high school and college those kinds of contacts were common. As a stay-at-home mom, I remember those informal connections with other moms. A major difference for me these days is being in the work world.

Like Jessica, my brother, Mark, who lives a healthy balance of work, family and friends, mourns the loss of the kinds of spontaneous friendships he had when he was younger. "Everything has to be planned," he said. "I remember those days when fun activities with friends just happened. You ran into someone in the hallway of the dorm and ended up playing basketball together. Now it's all scheduled, sometimes weeks in advance. We're juggling trips for work and family commitments, looking carefully for those moments when we can meet up as friends."

Both Jessica and Mark place high value on their friendships and work hard to nurture them. They place a high value on their families, both their nuclear and extended families, and they are careful that their work and other activities don't damage family relationships. But careful balance of work, family and friends takes a lot of scheduling and organization, which sometimes feels artificial and inconsistent with real relationships.

It's worth noting that neither Jessica nor Mark uses online social networking. Jessica longs for "snippets of conversation that feel more real." Many people find online some aspects of the casual, relaxed interchanges both Jessica and Mark value. A few months ago, one of my friends wrote to me, "It occurred to me that Facebook is a modern equivalent of friends dropping by for a brief visit (and it's okay if I'm in curlers!), or maybe even a bit like the old round-robin letters that my family used to do."

LIFE STAGE, BUSYNESS AND MOBILITY

Some busyness and mobility issues are related to a person's stage in life. For example, Janet, an accountant in her forties, was recently promoted to a managerial role. For the past three years, since she and her family moved to a new city, she had been working three-quarter time doing accounting work with clients. Now she oversees a team of accountants in addition to maintaining her own clients. With the promotion, her work hours increased to full time.

The timing was good. All her children are growing in independence. Her daughter will finish high school in two years, and her two sons attend the local university, with one of them still living at home. The extra money helps cover tuition costs.

However, Janet is aware of the downside of the promotion. Even when working three-quarter time, she always felt behind in her friendships. Being in a new city means that friendships require that extra bit of effort, and the energy just isn't there. She has met many women with whom she feels a connection, but she never has time to take initiative to make contact for coffee or lunch. After three years in a new city, she realizes her life revolves around her husband, her children and her work. Those are all important priorities, but what about friends?

Janet's pattern of relationships illustrates a trend that has been documented by researchers. On the average, women are working in paid employment many more hours each week than they did several decades ago. Because husbands need to help more with parenting and household chores, this reduces the total number of hours available each week for both men and women to volunteer and engage in outside activities. Because of a smaller network of relationships outside the home, relationships within the home have become more significant for discussion of important issues and for personal support.[1] For Janet, throw in the fact that she's in a new city, and the pattern is magnified.

In Janet's case, some of her time pressure comes from the fact that her career has escalated while she still has two children living at home. Five years or ten years from now, she will most likely have more time and energy for friendships after work.

Jerome and Dorothy, now in their early fifties, illustrate another friendship challenge related to the overlapping issues of life stage, busyness and mobility. They moved to a new city right before their first child was born. They moved again twenty years later, right about the time of the empty nest. They have been in that same place now for six years, but they have found friendships to be much slower to develop in their current city. "The friends we've made in recent years don't seem as close, somehow," Jerome said. "Part of it must be because they don't know our children except as visitors who drop into our lives occasionally. For us, our children are of central importance, but our friends now barely know them." Dorothy agreed.

> The friendships we made when our children were young seem deeper. Is it because we went through those stressful years of early parenthood together? Or was it because I was a stay-at-home mom, and I had a lot of time for friendships? I spent time at the children's school and with other families in the neighborhood, and those families became friends for Jerome as well. Now that I'm working, I have less time and energy to develop friendships.

I have a lot of compassion for Janet, Jerome and Dorothy. Meeting the friendship challenges related to our stage in life—challenges compounded by busyness and mobility—requires endurance, patience and perseverance, making the most of a hard

Friends Die

Maggie and I were close friends in college and shared an apartment for two years after college. She was the maid of honor in my wedding and godmother to my two sons. In our thirties we saw each other less often, but stayed in frequent contact. We were forty-one when she started getting headaches. They were caused by a brain tumor, and she died only a few months after the diagnosis. I cried at odd times for more than a year.

Five years after Maggie died, another friend got cancer. Not a close friend this time, but a friend nonetheless. I can remember sitting on the sofa in my living room, arguing with God. "I can't do this again! I can't lose another friend."

"Yes, you can. And you will. Many more times." I felt like God answered me in words that day, something that doesn't happen to me very often. The words weren't sympathetic. They were bracing.

God's words made me think of my great-aunt Lynn. She died in her early nineties, and toward the end of her life she told me how lonely she was. All her friends had died long before she did.

I'm not even close to my nineties, but God's words have come true. Friends die. It really hurts.

situation that may change with time. My paradigm of friendship as a verb would say to these three individuals that actions of friendship still matter. Even when time is limited, taking a few steps to nurture friends will bear fruit for later days when time may be more plentiful. And even when friendships are harder to come by and slower to develop, actions of friendship that reflect the love of God will ultimately bear fruit.

CHALLENGES FROM WITHIN

Martin, in his fifties, believes that one of the greatest challenges in friendship today is that we fear being known, even while we crave it. His conviction reflects an accurate perception that some friendship challenges come from our own choices and our own inability to act in ways that will ultimately nurture friendship.

Roberta, a social worker in her forties, spoke about the same issue: "I know that I need to spend more time nurturing friendships. My kids are leaving home, and my husband is going back to university to train in a new field. I'm going to be lonely in the years he's studying unless I building some more friendships. But I find it so difficult to talk about myself, what I'm thinking and feeling, what I'm struggling with. I fear saying too much about things inside me."

A story from my own life illustrates this reality. I have no close friends from high school, and that is no accident.

We moved from Virginia to Washington State the summer I turned fifteen, between junior high and high school. In junior high, I had watched the "popular" girls from afar, observing the way they flirted with boys and acted bored and flippant. In Virginia, I had been a serious piano student and a Girl Scout with lots of merit badges. I got almost all As in school, and my favorite haunt was the local library. Definitely not "popular."

When we moved to Washington, I decided to reinvent myself by pretending I had been popular in Virginia. I dropped Girl Scouts and joined the swim team because it seemed to have a lot of boys. I maintained a sophisticated, slightly mysterious air. Very soon some of the boys on the swim team started asking me out on dates. I made friends with girls who matched my new languid and superficial persona. We listened to rock music and talked about boys, clothes and makeup. We double-dated.

I couldn't sustain this new person I had created. By my second year of high school, I was slipping back into my old self. I grew apart from the girls I had become friends with. By the time I reached my third and last year of high school, I was back to my real self, serious, a bit nerdy, more interested in books than makeup and clothes.

But it was too late to make high-school friends based on my

true self. When I left Washington for a university in Oregon, I decided I would never again try to pretend to be anything other than myself. I didn't always succeed in being vulnerable and honest with friends, but I did pretty well. I still have several close friends from my college days, and those dear friends know me for who I am. And they actually like me. What a gift!

Perhaps I'm lucky that moving when I was fifteen gave me the opportunity to experiment with reinventing myself. My failed experiment left me with the conviction that I never again wanted to act a role. It was instrumental in giving me the courage to be myself in relationships, to reveal my thoughts and feelings, and to get over the fear of being known. That openness and vulnerability has enabled me to be "real" with people—sometimes too real—but it has generally been fruitful in friendships.

RELATIONSHIPS IN OUR TIME

Some of the challenges in relationships today come from the simple fact that our mobile world has created more relational connections than many of us are suited for. "I wonder if we are trying to have too many friends," said Dorothy, a university lecturer in her fifties. Dorothy has been helping her mother with some genealogical research. They have been rereading family reminiscences about Dorothy's great-grandmother, beginning in the 1860s, when she immigrated to New Zealand as a thirteen-year-old orphan, and extending for many decades.

It was evident from the family stories that, by today's standards, the circle of relationships more than a century ago was fairly small. Families were big with lots of children, so the extended family included several dozen people. In Dorothy's great-grandmother's case, that one family seems to have been connected through their lifetime to only a few other families. In some cases, the friendships seem to have involved only one or two people in those other families, and in other cases there were connections with many members of another extended family. But because towns were smaller and mobility was much more limited, those few other families made up the friendships for most of Dorothy's great-grandmother's adult life.

These days, most people juggle hundreds of relationships over a lifetime, using multiple means of sustaining connections. Careful consideration of how best to do that will be increasingly necessary.

Another friendship challenge today comes from the fact that most articles, books and talk shows that analyze relationships focus on romantic relationships, not friendships. Because of all the analysis of dating and romance, common patterns and markers of progress have been identified. While some of them may be a bit crude—"Did you get to first, second or third base on that date?"—markers of progress are easier to identify in dating relationships than in friendships.

In an online review of the movie *I Love You, Man*, Ezra Klein reflects on this reality:

> What the movie gets right, I think, is the way in which making friends as an adult is not merely similar to dating, but actually worse. The absence of sex renders the process *more* uncertain: Unlike with dating, there are few discrete waypoints available to help you judge the relationship's progression. Unlike with dating, the acceptable behaviors aren't rigidly defined and so the appropriate moves are not always as obvious. Even the expectations are more uncertain: Two single people at least have a certain symmetry in their dating lives. That's not true for two potential friends, one who might have lots of friends and a busy social calendar and the other who might be searching out a best friend or a whole new group.[2]

I've experienced this reality in the three years since I moved to New Zealand. Several times, I have felt awkward in friendships because I don't know the waypoints of friendships in this culture. To the extent that friendship markers exist in the United States, I have a pretty good grasp of them. But there are enough cultural differences between the United States and New Zealand that I'm not sure I'm reading the relational signs accurately here.

WHEN YOU DON'T LIKE YOUR FRIEND'S SPOUSE

Some friendship challenges result from specific situations. Several people talked to me with great emotion about their dislike for the spouse of a friend.

One man, in his forties, has let a close friendship slip away in recent years. His friend married a woman who cannot stop talking about herself. Every conversation comes back to her, and the man I interviewed found he just couldn't stand it. He was unable to nurture the friendship without involving his friend's wife, so he gradually stopped seeing his friend.

A man in his late thirties told me about his agony when his close friend recently married a woman who nags and criticizes her new husband. "I could see the pattern before they got married, and I wondered if I should say something," he said. "But I didn't. Now I'm trying to figure out how to stay friends when I can barely stand being in the same room with his wife."

A woman in her forties talked to me about two husbands of her friends whom she doesn't like. One of the husbands seems to be always convinced he's right. The other husband simply talks too much, dominating conversations. "I've wondered if something is wrong with me that I dislike these two men so much," she said. "Then I remind myself that I like husbands of most of my other friends just fine. I'm civil to these two husbands when I encounter them, but I never initiate gatherings that involve these husbands." She has managed to continue to nurture friendships with the two women through phone calls, lunches and gatherings just for women.

Numerous other specific situations create challenges for friends today. A friend who gets promoted and becomes a boss. A friend with a very different personality style that grates. Changes in job schedules or family situations.

Maybe these trying situations aren't the most significant cause of friendship challenges in our time. Is consumerism shaping us and damaging our friendships more than we acknowledge? Maybe friendship in our time is suffering less from the influx of new technology and the stress of mobility and busy schedules, and more from the consumeristic, commercial orientation to see everything—including "human resources"—as assets or liabilities. Maybe friendship is difficult today because we consider each other from a functional point of view, and we are ourselves too busy strengthening our personal brand and increasing our market share by "friending" everyone we meet.

God's relational nature and Jesus' invitation to be friends with him can shape and nurture human friendships. We are human beings, not human doings or merely consumers, and our being is rooted and grounded in the God who created us for relationship. In the next chapter we turn to a discussion of the God who calls us friends.

QUESTIONS FOR REFLECTION, JOURNALING, DISCUSSION OR ACTION

- What are your biggest friendship challenges that do not come from technology, perhaps challenges not mentioned in this chapter? With whom do you, or could you, talk about those challenges?

- Do you or have you struggled to be yourself, honestly and openly, in friendships? What has helped you grow in openness and vulnerability? In what ways would you like to grow in openness and vulnerability?

- Spend time meditating on Colossians 3:12-17 and 1 Corinthians 13. In what ways do these passages encourage you to face friendship challenges?

- What do you long for most of all in the area of friendship? In response to that longing, what have you done or what could you do? If you could ask someone to pray for you in the area of friendship, what would be the topic of the prayer? Write out a prayer that contains your dreams and desires for your friendships.

- Spend time praying about the challenges you currently experience in your friendships. Ask God for insight about the causes of those challenges, and ask for the wisdom to know how best to respond to them.

6

FRIENDSHIP WITH GOD

A friend is someone who knows all about you and likes you anyway, one who listens without telling and confides without withholding, who depends on you when the going is tough and laughs with you most of the time.

—Deborah, a retired teacher in her seventies

The supreme happiness of life is the conviction that we are loved for ourselves.

—Victor Hugo (1802–1885)

When I was nineteen or twenty, I came across the idea that human beings are created in God's image (see Genesis 1:26). I wondered what that meant, so I began asking older Christians I respected. The answer, given to me by several different people, was that humans are rational, like God is.

In the decades since I asked that question, Christian theologians have engaged in a burst of writing and thinking about the Trinity, emphasizing the intimate relationship between the persons of the Trinity.[1] What does it mean to be made in God's image? Today, many theologians would answer by saying that humans are created for relationships that mirror the relationship between God the Father, God the Son and God the Holy Spirit. Being made in God's image means that we are created to love and give and care. We are invited into intimacy with the triune God, the God of relationship, and we are invited into intimacy with each other.

I was in my mid-thirties when I first heard that revised answer to my burning question, and it was a giant *aha* moment for me. I had liked the previous answer. I had liked believing that what sets humans apart from animals is that we are rational. It made me feel a bit smug. I can do "rational" fairly easily most of the time.

Pondering the image of God in humans as a call to relationship didn't make me feel smug. It made me feel challenged. It called me to be my best self, to let go of selfishness and grudges and pride. It said to me that using my rationality and intelligence as ends in themselves might be a good thing, but using my rationality and intelligence and other gifts to serve people and nurture connections with them is infinitely more important.

GOD AS FRIEND

I had another *aha* moment about ten years later. I was sitting in a rental car at a California beach on a blustery winter afternoon, reading the Bible, on my circuitous way from the airport to a conference. I read John 15:12-17, a passage that was familiar to me. This time I saw it in a new light. On his last night with his disciples before his death and resurrection, Jesus said,

> This is my commandment, that you love one another as I have loved you. No one has greater love than this, to lay down one's life for one's friends. You are my friends if you do what I command you. I do not call you servants any longer, because the servant does not know what the master is doing; but I have called you friends, because I have made known to you everything that I have heard from my Father. You did not choose me but I chose you. And I appointed you to go and bear fruit, fruit that will last, so that the Father will give you whatever you ask him in my name. I am giving you these commands so that you may love one another.

Jesus calls us his friends! For some reason, on that day, the impact of that statement stunned me. I sat in my rented car in the

cold wind, watching the pounding waves, pondering the significance of this invitation to friendship.

Friends have a level of equality with each other, and Jesus affirms
that he can call us friends because he has revealed what his Father is
doing, so we're not in the dark about God's purposes and plans. Yet
this friendship is characterized by obedience as well. We are com-
manded to obey Jesus, but the command here is really more of an invitation. Jesus invites us to enter into this new thing that the Father is doing and that Jesus is making known.

> O worship the King all glorious above,
>
> O gratefully sing His power and His love;
>
> Our Shield and Defender, the Ancient of Days,
>
> Pavilioned in splendor, and girded with praise.
>
> Frail children of dust, and feeble as frail,
>
> In Thee do we trust, nor find Thee to fail;
>
> Thy mercies how tender, how firm to the end,
>
> Our Maker, Defender, Redeemer, and Friend.
>
> *ROBERT GRANT, 1833, based on Psalm 103*

In these verses, Jesus' command to obey him is an invitation into the relationship he has with his Father, a relationship
of obedience and submission. Jesus submits to his Father, and we
submit to Jesus, a submission in both cases characterized by
knowledge of what the Father is doing, not blind obedience. This
submission is part of a loving, caring, intimate relationship.

In fact, Jesus invites us into the friendship he has with the one
he calls Father. My two *aha* moments are connected to each other.
We are created in the image of a God who lives in love: the three
persons of the Trinity eternally intimate with and devoted to each
other. That love spills over to us. We are loved, and we are called
to love. We are invited into friendship with this God, and Jesus
Christ is the one who makes that friendship possible by dying to
reconcile us to God.

Throughout the ages, numerous Christian theologians and
writers have described salvation in Christ as entering into friendship with God. In fact, in John 15, Jesus talks about laying his life

down as a significant component of his friendship with us. Beautiful hymns and poems, dating from almost every century of Christian history, describe friendship with God and often relate that friendship to salvation in Christ.

FRIENDSHIP WITH CHRIST AND FRIENDSHIP WITH OTHERS

What difference does it make for human friendships that we are invited to be friends with Christ? First and foremost, if our human friendships mirror that intimacy between the three persons of the Trinity, as well as reflecting the friendship between Jesus and humans, then we aren't inventing friendship. Instead we are entering into something that is already happening and something that was patterned into us at creation because of the fact that we are made in God's image. Yes, the world is broken. Yes, the image of God in human beings is blurred by sin. But even though those things are true, as we grow in maturity as human beings, we grow in our ability to love and care for others. We were made for relationships; being relational was etched into us when we were made.

Second, we can expect that a relationship with God through Jesus Christ will help us grow in our ability to nurture human friendships. God's business is relationships. Love is the hallmark of God's personality and priorities. As we draw near to that God, the Holy Spirit will help us to grow in love, which will spill over to all our relationships. We don't have to strain to have human friendships. God will help us forgive, share, reach out and show compassion and kindness. We can draw near to God and expect that, over time, our ability to live in communal love with others will grow because of God's Spirit at work within us.

The relationality of the Trinity isn't just something we are called upon to emulate; it is actually something we are gathered into. Like the shepherd gathering the lost sheep, Jesus comes to find us, comes looking for us so that he might gather us into the embrace of the divine love. When we love others, we are resting in the embrace of that love. We don't have to generate the love. It is already there.

When we grow in friendship with Christ, when we allow ourselves to be Jesus' friends and allow ourselves to receive his love, we will find it easier to pass that love on to others. We love because God first loved us (see 1 John 4:19). So many conflicts between friends grow out of insecurity and pride. The more we know deep inside that we are loved, the more we rest in the embrace of the God who loves us, the more secure we will feel and the less we will need to bolster our pride. As we receive love from God, we will feel increasingly peaceful and harmonious internally, and that peace and harmony will spill over into relationships with others.

> Alleluia! Sing to Jesus!
> His the scepter, his the throne;
> Alleluia! His the triumph,
> His the victory alone;
> Hark! the songs of peaceful Zion
> thunder like a mighty flood;
> Jesus out of every nation
> hath redeemed us by his blood.
>
> Alleluia! Bread of angels,
> Thou on earth our food, our stay!
> Alleluia! here the sinful
> Flee to thee from day to day:
> Intercessor, Friend of sinners,
> Earth's Redeemer, plead for me,
> Where the songs of all the sinless
> Sweet across the crystal sea.
>
> WILLIAM CHATTERTON DIX, 1866

WHO IS MY NEIGHBOR?

The story in Luke 10:25-37 about the good Samaritan is one of the best-loved stories of the Bible. The story and Jesus' words before and after he tells it provide helpful teaching about the kind of intentionality in friendship to which God calls us.

Most readers focus on the drama in the story: the man who is beaten up and robbed, the people who pass by on the other side of the road and the Samaritan who unexpectedly gives aid and demonstrates care and concern across cultural and ethnic boundaries. I love the story in itself, but I've always been equally interested in the circumstances of when and why Jesus told it.

The story follows the return of the seventy, who have been sent out by Jesus to preach and heal. After the disciples come back and debrief with Jesus, an expert in the law "stood up to test Jesus." He asks what he should do to inherit eternal life.

Jesus replied, "What is written in the law? What do you read there?"

The man answered, "You shall love the Lord your God with all your heart, and with all your soul, and with all your strength, and with all your mind; and your neighbor as yourself."

Jesus tells him he has given the right answer. The man then asks, "Who is my neighbor?"

At that point, Jesus tells the story of the good Samaritan and ends the story by asking the expert in the law which character in the story was a neighbor to the man who was robbed. The answer is obvious, and the man responds, "The one who showed him mercy."

When the man asked, "Who is my neighbor?" he was asking who he should consider as a neighbor. After Jesus told the story, he asked who had acted like a neighbor. Jesus shifted the emphasis of the question. The expert in the law was asking him to define a category of people, the people who fit into this group called "neighbor." Jesus instead emphasized a category of actions, the actions that are neighborly.

Our task, Jesus is implying, is not to figure out who fits into the category of neighbor so we can love them. Instead our challenge is to figure out when and how to act in a neighborly fashion, how to be a neighbor.

FRIENDSHIP AS ACTION

The story of the good Samaritan has profound implications for friendship. The challenge in friendship isn't to figure out who is a friend. The challenge is to grow in ability to act like a friend. The remainder of this book will explore the kinds of intentional practices that help us grow in our ability to be a friend.

These intentional practices are rooted in the understanding that human friendship is an invitation to participate in the love that the three persons of the Trinity have for each other and the love that the triune God has for us. That love is most visible in Jesus Christ, who lived and died for us, and was raised from the dead to undo the forces of hate and evil in the world. That love is made real in our lives through the work of the Holy Spirit. When we read the description of love in 1 Corinthians 13, those characteristics don't come out of a vacuum. They come from God, are best exemplified in the person of Jesus Christ and are made real through the work of the Holy Spirit.

Scholars often point out that in some ways 1 Corinthians 13 is a commentary on the life of Jesus. He alone is the one who defines love as this sort of love: patient, kind, rejoicing in the truth, bearing all things, believing all things, hoping all things and enduring all things. In Jesus, love never fails or ends. The four Gospels are full of stories that demonstrate the kind of love that reaches beyond itself and enters into another person's world. To give just a few examples, Jesus touched a leper, talked with a Samaritan woman at length and set a crippled woman free from bondage (see Mark 1:41; John 4; Luke 13:10-17). All these actions required the ability to empathize with and enter into the other person's emotions and situation.

Not only does Jesus exemplify this kind of love, he also enables us to love like this as we are remade in his image. Our ability to put on this kind of love, to clothe ourselves with it, comes first from clothing ourselves in Christ (see Romans 13:14; Galatians 3:27). Being clothed with Christ, putting on Christ, is a powerful metaphor for salvation, and clothing ourselves with Christ will enable us to grow in loving like he loves.

Jesus is our friend as the Savior of the world. Jesus is our friend as the one who lays down his life for his friends. Jesus invites us to follow him, to be the kind of friends who stick around when times are tough for others, to be the kind of friends who give and care and reach beyond ourselves. The depth of friendship we are offered in Jesus can be a foundation for friendship with the people we love.

The apostle Paul wrote, "As God's chosen ones, holy and beloved, clothe yourselves with compassion, kindness, humility, meekness, and patience. . . . Above all, clothe yourselves with love, which binds everything together in perfect harmony" (Colossians 3:12, 14). We'll be able to put on that clothing most easily when we know deeply and profoundly that we're chosen and beloved by God.

Love is the belt buckle that holds on the new clothing that Paul describes in Colossians 3. The characteristics of the new clothing—compassion, kindness, humility, meekness and patience—aren't utilitarian. They aren't primarily a means to an end, although they do result in very good things. Instead they are rooted and established in love, the love that flows from God. They are a reflection of a deep and profound reality: the love of God for the creatures he made and holds in his hands.

Note the circle this creates. Paul calls us to compassion, kindness, humility, meekness and patience, which are all bound up in love, which we learn from 1 Corinthians 13 is itself patient, kind and so on. We are clothed in loving patience when we are patient in our loving; we are clothed in loving kindness when we are kind in our

> My song is love unknown,
>
> My Savior's love to me,
>
> Love to the loveless shown,
>
> That they might lovely be.
>
> O who am I,
>
> That for my sake
>
> My Lord should take frail flesh and die?
>
> He came from his blest throne,
>
> Salvation to bestow,
>
> But men made strange and none
>
> The longed for Christ would know.
>
> But O, My friend,
>
> My Friend indeed,
>
> Who at my need his life should spend!
>
> Here might I stay and sing,
>
> No story so divine;
>
> Never was love, dear King,
>
> Never was grief like Thine.
>
> This is my Friend,
>
> In whose sweet praise
>
> I all my days could gladly spend.
>
> *SAMUEL CROSSMAN (c. 1624–1683)*

loving. We become what we clothe ourselves in, and we clothe ourselves in our habits.

Let me say my main point again: The challenge in friendship isn't to figure out who is a friend. The challenge is to grow in the ability to act like a friend.

Throughout the ages, wise people have asserted that the way to have friends is to be a friend. Let's explore some of the ways to grow in the actions that make us faithful friends.

QUESTIONS FOR REFLECTION, JOURNALING, DISCUSSION OR ACTION

- Spend some time pondering John 15:12-17. What do you find most comforting about the passage? Most challenging? What questions do you have about the passage? What do you think is the connection between friendship with Jesus and obedience to him?

- In what ways have you experienced Jesus to be your friend? In what ways would you like to grow in friendship with Jesus? What are some steps you might take to grow in friendship with him? In what ways might friendship with Jesus help you be a better friend?

- Spend time meditating on the words of the hymns and poems in the sidebars of this chapter. What connections between salvation in Christ and friendship with Christ do you see there? What do you see about friendship with Jesus in the hymns and poems that connects with your own life?

- Do you agree that the central challenge in friendship is to grow in the ability to act like a friend? Why or why not? Do your friendship patterns reflect your convictions in this area?

- This week, ask two or three people about the ways they experience Jesus as their friend. What do you like about their responses? What do you disagree with?

- Spend time praying about your own experience of Jesus as your friend, and spend time praying about the ways you seek to act like a friend to others. Ask God for discernment to see the factors that influence your experience in both areas, and ask for the wisdom to know how to respond.

7

INITIATING

Good friends are caring, loyal and understanding. They're strong, so you can lean on them. They have integrity, so you know that what you tell them won't go any further. They have time for you, and they make connection with you at least sometimes, so it's not always you who has to take initiative.

—Tabitha, in her eighties

The greatest weakness of most humans is their hesitancy to tell others how much they love them while they're still alive.

—Orlando A. Battista (1917–1995)

When I think of *friendship* as a verb, when I think of actions that shape friendship, what comes to mind first and foremost is the willingness to take initiative. Over and over.

Initiative means making some kind of response after a friend has surgery. Perhaps a card, a meal, a gift, a phone call or a visit. Initiative means creating opportunities to listen when a friend is going through a crisis—suggesting a conversation over coffee, making time for a phone call or sending an email with specific questions about the situation. Initiative means checking in with friends when you haven't heard from them for a while. Initiative means remembering to pray for a friend's needs.

I know that initiative is so important to me because I had to navigate eleven moves in my first fifteen years. As I look back on my childhood, I can see clearly that if I hadn't taken initiative over and over to reach out to potential new friends, I would have been desperately lonely.

The emphasis I place on initiating in friendship also comes from conversations I've had with both men and women over the years. "I have trouble initiating," many people have told me as they talk about feeling isolated and wanting more friends. Initiative in our time takes many forms, and we'll consider a variety of kinds of initiative in this chapter. We'll also explore some of the obstacles to initiating.

WHAT MARY MIGHT HAVE MISSED

One of my favorite friendship stories in the Bible reveals an act of initiative that is easy to miss. Luke 1 and 2 describes the miracle pregnancies of two cousins, Elizabeth and Mary, and the friendship that grows between them.

Elizabeth and her husband were getting on in years, and they had no child. In a series of dramatic events, God reveals to Elizabeth's husband that they will have a child who will have a significant role in God's plan. That son will be John the Baptist.

Mary is also pregnant with a miracle baby, Jesus. The angel Gabriel gives Mary the news that she will bear a son who will be called "the Son of the Most High" (Luke 1:32). After Mary asks how this can happen, given that she is a virgin, Gabriel explains that the Holy Spirit will make it possible. Then Gabriel says, "And now, your relative Elizabeth in her old age has also conceived a son; and this is the sixth month for her who was said to be barren. For nothing will be impossible with God" (Luke 1:36-37).

Immediately after the conversation with the angel, Mary sets out on a visit to her cousin. She stays with Elizabeth three months, and we can only imagine the comfort these two women gave to each other. They undoubtedly talked over the miraculous events surrounding the conception of their babies. They probably shared their fears about the lives their sons would lead and the impact of

God's call on each of them. According to Luke, Mary is in Elizabeth's presence when she says the famous prayer often called the
Magnificat, a prayer beloved by Christians for two thousand years
(see Luke 1:46-55).

What we so easily miss is the fact that the angel did not tell
Mary to visit Elizabeth. Gabriel simply announced that Elizabeth
was pregnant after waiting so long. Mary chose to go visit. Her
willingness to take initiative in this way nurtured the friendship
between her and Elizabeth and benefited both of them.

I can imagine another scenario that could very easily have happened if Mary hadn't taken that initiative. In my alternative story,
Mary stays home. The angel tells her that Elizabeth is pregnant,
and Mary is happy to hear it. She tells her mother about it, and
maybe local female cousins as well, and they spend a lot of time
talking about how wonderful it is for Elizabeth to be pregnant.
They tell each other stories of women they knew who struggled
with infertility. They talk about women who became pregnant
after giving up hope. Perhaps they refer to Abraham and Sarah
from the Bible, or maybe they remember Hannah, another biblical
character who became pregnant after waiting a long time.[1] Pregnancy after infertility is a wonderful gift, and, just like today,
probably everyone in Mary's village had a story to tell about it.

But Elizabeth's pregnancy, blessing as it was, had additional
significance beyond the gift of a baby after a long period of infertility. Elizabeth's son would grow up to be "great in the sight of the
Lord" and would speak and minister "with the spirit and power of
Elijah" (Luke 1:15, 17). If Mary hadn't taken the initiative to visit
Elizabeth, she would have missed talking with the one woman
who had some inkling of the amazing thing that had happened to
her and the high calling of her son.

After Jesus is born, Joseph and Mary present him in the temple.
A faithful man named Simeon recognizes that Jesus is the Mes-
siah. He says a beautiful prayer in response to seeing Jesus, and
then turns to Mary and tells her what he sees about Jesus' minis-

try. His final words to Mary are sobering: "A sword will pierce your own soul" (Luke 2:35).

Mary's conversations with Elizabeth may very well have given her the foundation for the kind of strength and resilience she would need in order to live with that sword piercing her heart. Because of her visit with Elizabeth, she entered into her role as mother of the Son of God knowing she was not alone in bearing a miracle baby who would be called to do extraordinary things.

We have no record of Elizabeth and Mary meeting again. When horrible things happened to John the Bapist and then later to Jesus, the memory of those three months with Elizabeth must have given Mary comfort. Mary would have known that one other woman had been called by God to bear a child who would change history and who would bring tears and great sadness to his mother.

OBSTACLES TO INITIATING

In my alternative scenario, Mary stays home instead of setting out to visit Elizabeth. Why might Mary have made that decision? She might have stayed home if she had wondered if Elizabeth would welcome her. She might have stayed home if she had a lot of fears about what might happen on the journey. She might have felt obligated to help her mother or take care of her younger siblings, and her sense of responsibility might have kept her at home.

In the same way, many people today find it hard to initiate with friends or potential friends because of wondering if the act of initiative will be welcome. Many people have fears about the whole process of taking action. Will something bad or unpleasant happen? And many people are so absorbed with immediate needs—household, family, work—that they find it hard to think about extending a gesture of friendship to someone who is not immediately present.

"Love is kind." Love "believes all things, hopes all things" (1 Corinthians 13:4, 7). Part of the solution to the fears of reaching out in friendship comes from considering how to love the people with whom we are friends or with whom we might start a friendship. What would it look like to act in kindness to someone we know? What would it look like to believe and hope that our kindness will be received? Or to believe and hope that kindness is never wasted, that God will bring good things from it whether or not it is received graciously by the person to whom it is given?

> Talk not of wasted affection; affection never was wasted.
> If it enrich not the heart of another, its waters returning
> Back to their springs, like the rain shall fill them full of refreshment;
> That which the fountain sends forth returns again to the fountain.
>
> *HENRY WADSWORTH LONGFELLOW (1807–1882)*

When we reach out in kindness toward a friend or potential friend, we are mirroring the love of God that reaches into our lives. When we act in kindness with the hope of a positive response, but with the willingness to show love even if the response is tepid or negative, we are reflecting the character of God. The kind of initiative that builds true friendships is rooted in God's love, full of kindness and hope, believing the best outcome may be possible.

Love carries its own reward. When we act in love, when we take initiative to show kindness and compassion, we are mirroring the character of God as shown to us in Jesus Christ. Every time we do that, we are participating in God's work of transformation in us. Even if our act of kindness isn't received very enthusiastically, we will be blessed if we trust that God's love is shaping us into the people we were created to be.

OVERCOMING FEAR

The fear of initiating is a significant obstacle in friendship. If I call and invite someone to get together with me, will I be rebuffed? If I ask someone over for dinner, will they hate the food I fix? Will my house be too messy? Will conversation lag? Isn't it better just to wait until someone takes initiative with me?

Damon, a nurse in his late forties, has been working on initiating in friendships for the past twenty years. He has come to view it as one of the tasks required for his spiritual growth.

I remember being an adolescent and a teenager. It seemed like there was always something to do. There were plenty of boys in my neighborhood, and we played baseball and basketball all the time. Then I went off to college, and the other guys in the dorm were always up for a movie or a game of tennis. It just seemed to happen. I didn't have to take action myself in order to have friends.

Then I grew up and got a job. I was the only male nurse, so I was lonely at work. My roommates were busy working, and I didn't know how to find people to do things with. In my family growing up, the mantra was "What will the neighbors say?" There was a lot of shame and fear. My parents seldom invited people over to our house because they were worried someone would take offense at the food they served or the way we lived. My dad had friends from work, but my mom was very isolated because of her fear.

When I met my wife, I was so surprised to find that she came from a family where both her parents had a lot of friends. They had people over for meals, they visited friends when they went on vacation, they sent a bazillion Christmas cards every year. I watched my wife handle her friendships. She was always taking initiative in some way, sending a card, calling someone up, inviting people over. I realized I had never learned how to do that. So I started trying. I realized that if I wanted to show Christ's love to the people I knew and if I wanted to have friends, I had to learn to take initiative.

It felt so awkward at first. Twenty years later, I'm still learning. But it comes more easily than it did before, and I have friends now. Good friends. Real friends. And I see that reaching out to people is a part of being a loving person, which has the side effect of nurturing friendships as well. And it brings great joy to me in the process.

About a decade ago, Damon reconnected with his cousins on his father's side of the family. They live on the other side of the country. In the past ten years, he has seen them in person a few times at family gatherings and funerals, and he has emailed off and on with them, feeling increasingly close to them. Recently his cousin Betsy had a stroke. Damon found out about it through an email Betsy sent to friends and relatives. He emailed back, saying he was praying for her.

One morning, a few weeks after Betsy's stroke, Damon woke up thinking about her. She stayed on his mind through breakfast and into the morning. He decided those thoughts might be a nudge from God that he should phone her.

She was at home alone and delighted to hear from him. In the first couple of weeks after the stroke, family members and friends from her church had been coming to help her every day, but now she was alone. Damon's call was a lifeline for her that day, and when they hung up, she said to him, "You're a sweetheart."

The words warmed his heart, particularly in the light of his long journey to learn to initiate with friends. Listening to those nudges from God is playing an increasingly significant role for him as he continues to grow in intentionality in friendships.

Damon's story illustrates the encouraging reality that taking initiative in friendship can be learned. It takes time and effort, but in recent years Damon has experienced increased ease in reaching out to friends and potential friends in a number of ways.

DIFFERENT WAYS OF INITIATING

Imagine that your friend has been studying part time for several years to get a particular academic degree. Graduation is coming up in a few months, and you want to do something to congratulate your friend for the hard work and strategic juggling that has resulted in this achievement.

Should you buy a gift? Send a card? Offer to take photos at the graduation ceremony? Invite your friend over for a meal? Offer to host a party? Offer to take your friend out to a favorite restaurant to celebrate? Invite your friend out for coffee and offer to be a sounding board for the next steps in his or her life?

Friendship, Time and Initiative

Serena, a librarian in her fifties, expressed two important beliefs: *Friendship takes time* **and** *to be friends requires intentionality; it rarely "happens."* **She noted that people so often say, "Let's get together," but find it hard to follow through. "I wouldn't have either," she said, "had I not scribbled notes to myself on my calendar or scraps of paper in my car to 'call this person' or 'invite that person over for dinner.'"**

Serena has nurtured the habit over the years of having people over for tea or dinner, either individually or in groups, and in this way has developed friendships with neighbors, coworkers and church members.

Serena believes work patterns profoundly influence friendships. "Not many people have the time—or want to make the time—to develop friendships. In families with children where both parents work full time outside the home, I have observed this to be very true. Part-time work, if one or both parents can afford it, is a real boon to friendship. It gives people breathing space."

What is the best way to initiate? Sometimes our ability to initiate is limited by our circumstances. If you are on a limited budget, you can't buy a lavish present or invite your friend out to a glitzy restaurant. If you live in a tiny apartment, you can't offer to host a party. If you've listened to your friend talk endlessly about the future, and you're so fed up with listening that you'll scream if you do it one minute more, you probably shouldn't invite your friend out for coffee and another listening session.

Joanne, a hospital human services manager in her forties, believes that observing her friends' love languages has helped her show love in appropriate and effective ways. She is referring to the many books by Gary D. Chapman about the five love languages.[2] Chapman believes that most of us have favorite ways to give and receive love, and he calls them "love languages." He identifies five of those languages: gifts, touch, undivided attention, words of affirmation and actions.

More than twenty years ago, my husband and I read an article by Chapman describing the five love languages, several years before his first book came out. The article stimulated a lot of conversation between my husband and me, and among our married friends at the time. It was easy for me to see that undivided attention—being listened to deeply and carefully—is the primary way I feel loved. I'm also very fond of being touched physically. I enjoy giving and receiving gifts, I enjoy receiving compliments and words of praise, and I enjoy being served. But if I don't feel I'm being listened to, I don't feel loved, even if I get hugs, gifts, compliments or actions that serve me.

As we talked about these love languages, my husband realized he feels most loved when I do something with him, whether it's an outing to an art gallery or working alongside him on a home repair. We don't necessarily need to be talking for him to feel loved in that way, and I don't really need to do anything other than be there with him. This doesn't fit into one of Chapman's five love languages, so we came to believe that companionship, at least in our marriage, is one more language of love.

Joanne believes the love languages are just as relevant to friendship as to marriage. "So much miscommunication comes from not knowing a person's love language," she said. She watches her friends, trying to notice the way they give love to her and to others, and she tries to show love to them the same way. "I have a friend whose love language is service. I try to do things for her, help her with household tasks, even though it doesn't come easily for me."

I can look back on many friendships and realize that I probably erred by not paying attention to the other person's love language. I mostly show love to friends by listening to them, because I value being listened to. I can remember someone from several decades ago who was obviously trying to be my friend. She was always buying me little things, which seemed irrelevant and even a bit pushy to me. I wish I had understood the significance of love languages in friendship back then so that I could have received her kindness and care in the spirit in which it was given. Instead I found myself wishing she would listen to me.

It would have been good if I could have engaged in some reflection like this: *Hmmm. She keeps giving me these annoying little gifts of no consequence. I wonder why such a pointless gesture is so captivating to her. Maybe she wishes people would think of her more often when she's not around? Maybe I should give her a little gift every once in a while, just to show her that she's in my thoughts.*

Or perhaps another kind of initiative would have been appropriate. *Hmmm. She seems to miss the point that I want to be paid attention to, but she must like me, because she keeps buying me stuff. Maybe we should have a conversation about this—define the relationship a little more.* Taking initiative to ask some questions about patterns of giving and receiving love, and about her hopes for our relationship, would have been a gift to her. I regret that I was not able to give that gift.

VULNERABILITY AS INITIATIVE

When I think of taking initiative in friendships, I think first of asking people to do things with me: have a meal at a restaurant or at my home, have coffee and talk, go to a movie, go for a walk. I also think of forms of initiative that involve communication: picking up the phone to make a call, sending an email or a Facebook message, writing a card.

When I asked Clare, eighteen, what she believed to be the best advice about nurturing friendships, she said, "Stay in close touch. Stay connected." She talked about all the acts of initiative she engages in with her friends. She tries to send frequent text messages, and she interacts often on Facebook by posting comments about her friends' photos, links and updates. She views those acts of connection as the foundation for good conversations when she sees her friends face-to-face.

Roberta, in her forties, brought up another form of initiative:

> I have trouble talking honestly about what I'm thinking and feeling. I know it has had a significant impact on my ability to make friends. I always appreciate it when others show vulnerability in a conversation, because it helps me get over the hurdle of talking honestly.

I've noticed that if I share some small vulnerability with someone I'd like to get to know better, they often respond by sharing something that matters to them as well. I might talk about something that's making me sad, something that's worrying me or something I've been thinking about a lot. I save my deep feelings of sadness or worry for my husband or my close friends, who I know I can trust to listen with sensitivity to what I'm feeling. With people who I don't know as well, I share feelings that are real but not particularly deep.

Part of that sharing is a bit of a test. I watch to see how they will respond. If they are able to enter into what I feel, and perhaps later share feelings of their own, I have some optimism that we might become deeper friends. I also see that sharing as an act of love, giving them the unspoken message that I'd be happy to listen to them talk about what they're thinking and feeling. They may not want me to listen to their inner concerns in that moment, but my openness extends an invitation for later conversations.

Initiative takes many forms, and we need to think creatively about it. My mother, an expert in friendship, takes initiative to reach out in some form to one or more friends almost every day of her life.

A GIFT GIVEN TO ME BY INITIATIVE

I am still awed by the gift I received when I took the initiative a few years ago to visit a friend named Shelagh (a Scottish name pronounced like "Sheila"). I met her when I was twenty-seven and she was twenty-one. My husband, Dave, and I were living in Tel Aviv, Israel, for eighteen months while he was filling in for someone at the university who was on sabbatical. Soon after our arrival, we met Shelagh at church. She was from South Africa and had been posted to her country's embassy in Tel Aviv as a secretary.

We discovered that Shelagh liked to play tennis just as much as Dave did, so we often met for tennis games. I watched while they played. What a pleasure! Shelagh was the most elegant tennis player I have ever seen. Her mother had played at Wimbledon, so Shelagh had had a tennis racket in her hand since childhood. After Shelagh beat Dave soundly, the three of us would have dinner together and talk.

Shelagh was one of those joyful, radiant Christians whose faith was encouraging and stimulating to me. She had a purity of heart that I admired very much.

When we moved back to Seattle after our time in Israel, Shelagh was posted to the South African Embassy in New York City for three years. We visited her one time there, and she spent a Christmas with us in Seattle. Then she was posted to Italy, where she met an Italian man, got married and had a son. She and I exchanged Christmas cards every year, and when email became common in the 1990s, we began to exchange prayer requests by email from time to time.

In 2006, Dave and I were planning a trip to Scandinavia. Dave also wanted to spend a few days with his cousin in Berlin. I didn't want to go to Berlin, so I thought I might use the time to visit some good friends who live in London. However, the more I thought about those three days, the more I felt nudged to visit Shelagh in Italy. I wrote to her, she was eager for me to come, so we set up the trip.

I hadn't seen her for twenty-four years, but it was like we had never been apart. Her purity of faith and joy in Christ had remained. I met her husband and son, and she showed me around Milan and cooked fabulous Italian food for me. On one memorable afternoon, we sat in a pew in the lofty and ornate Milan cathedral and prayed at length for our families.

One of the topics of conversation during my visit was Shelagh's future. Her son was nearing the end of high school. She had devoted herself to being a wife and mother, but she could see that her son would soon fly the nest. What was she going to do with her time after her son left home? We tossed around a few ideas, but nothing seemed to stick in her mind.

Now, looking back on those precious days in 2006, I can see why nothing appealed to Shelagh. God was preparing her for heaven. In 2007, she was diagnosed with stage-three ovarian cancer, and after surgery and two rounds of chemotherapy, she died eighteen months after her diagnosis.

I had felt nudged to go to Italy to see Shelagh, and I went. I am so glad. In the planning stages, though, I wasn't sure I was making the right decision. I wondered if it was crazy to go visit someone I hadn't seen for twenty-four years. I wondered if three days was too long. I wondered if it was a wise use of money. I wondered if it would be an imposition to her husband and son for me to be there. And, in fact, it was. Her son gave up his bedroom for me and had to sleep on a sofa in the TV room.

I felt nudged, and I went. And I will always be grateful. Shelagh was a bright spirit, a memorable person. Having those days together, less than a year before her cancer diagnosis, feels like a miracle.

When God nudges us to reach out to a friend or potential friend in any way—with a visit, a phone call, a conversation on Skype, a card, an email, a message on a social-networking website, a gift, a word of affirmation or love, an invitation to come over for a meal or to meet for coffee—we need to pay attention. Yes, we may feel a little or a lot of anxiety that our overture will not be welcome.

Some of that anxiety might prove to be justified. The unfortunate reality is that we may receive a less-than-enthusiastic response. In my experience, however, initiative is never wasted, even if it feels that way. Over time, acts of initiative shape our heart by training us to act in love.

Imagine a baseball player who stops swinging at pitches because he doesn't always connect with the ball. Imagine a basketball player who stops attempting to shoot baskets because she sometimes misses. That would be crazy, because no one hits a baseball or swishes a basketball every time. In the same way, every act of relational initiative will not result in a new friendship or make an existing friendship stronger. But some of them will.

We could carry the sports analogy further. It takes time and practice to learn which pitches to swing at and which ones to ignore. It takes time and practice to make good judgments about when to shoot a basket. In the same way, it takes time and practice to learn how to initiate in friendships. Even the most experienced athletes miss a lot of hits and baskets. But as they keep swinging a bat and shooting a ball, they grow in skill.

So many people have talked to me about the fears and obstacles they experience in initiating with friends. They seem frozen, like a baseball player who watches the ball coming and never swings or a basketball player who keeps dribbling and passing, but never shoots. Initiating requires practice, perseverance and willingness to risk. It requires the willingness to fail. Initiating in relationships mirrors the God who initiates with us, and whenever we reflect God, we are clothing ourselves in Christ and clothing ourselves in the love that comes from him.

Throughout the rest of the book, we'll be looking at a variety of habits that foster friendships, but at the base of every friendship, and infused throughout, is this core characteristic of initiative. Long before we experience the joys of friendship, we take actions to be a friend. In fact, without taking the initiative of friending, there can be no friendship.

QUESTIONS FOR REFLECTION, JOURNALING, DISCUSSION OR ACTION

- What models did you have in childhood for taking initiative in friendships? What are some acts of initiative that friends have taken with you that were particularly meaningful? How do those memories affect you now?

- Do you have fears around initiating in friendships? What are some of those fears? How do you typically respond?

- What forms of initiative in friendships come most easily to you? Which forms of initiative are hard? In what ways might God be inviting you to grow in this area?

- Which love language or languages are most comfortable for you to give and to receive? Analyze your patterns of initiating in friendships through the lens of the love languages. When you take initiative in friendship, do you overuse the languages of love that are more comfortable for you?

- This week, take initiative with a friend or potential friend in a way that is new for you. Watch how it feels for you.

- Spend time praying about the role of initiative in the way you practice friendship. Ask God for insight to understand why you do what you do, and ask God for help to grow in your ability to initiate wisely and with love.

8

LISTENING · REMEMBERING · PRAYING

Friendship is a mutual relationship of acceptance of each other as we are. It is a deep listening to the other's story of the joys and sorrows of life. It is experiencing empathy from the other, whether one agrees or not about particular issues of concern. It is being available to communicate with the other, especially in times of trouble.
—Adam, a retired minister in his sixties

Attention is the rarest and purest form of generosity.
—Simone Weil (1909–1943)

When I interviewed dozens of people for this book, the first question I asked was how they would define *friend* and *friendship*. I was amazed—and pleased—at the number of definitions I heard that included listening in some form or the other. I have always believed that listening is an essential friendship skill and that choosing to be an attentive listener is a form of intentionality that bears rich fruit in friendships. The interviews confirmed that belief.

For example, Layla, a twenty-year-old student, said,

> The biggest challenge to friendship is being selfish with friends. You think that friendship is a place where you can talk about yourself and your problems all the time. It's easy to think about what you can get from a friend, not what you can give. You need to sit and listen, not giving advice, but allowing the person to talk. You need to be able to drop every-

thing and give your friend time. I think we all take for granted how much effort it takes to keep a good friendship.

In recent years, I've been collecting listening skills. I've been observing what makes a person a good—or bad—listener. I thought that perhaps I place more emphasis on listening in friendship than others do because my primary language of love is undivided attention. But I came to the conclusion that whatever a person's language of love, there will always be times they need a listening ear.

As I've been collecting listening skills, I've watched the way some people do a great job using body language to indicate they're listening: eye contact, nodding, leaning a bit forward, showing attentiveness with their body. I've watched the way others use nonverbal sounds to indicate their willingness to hear more. "Mmmmm." "Hmmm." "Uh-huh."

Sometimes a word of affirmation for what the person has said will encourage him or her to keep talking. "I see what you mean." "I can understand how you'd feel that way." "Wow, that sounds amazing!"

Sometimes a listener issues an invitation to the person to keep talking. "Tell me more." Sometimes the invitation encourages the speaker to go deeper. "How did you feel when that happened?"

Books on active listening suggest reflecting back to a friend what you've heard her or him say. "It sounds like you're saying you were more scared than you'd ever been before." It can feel awkward to do that as a listener, but when you're the one describing something significant, it's like balm for the soul to know that your friend has truly heard you.

All of these listening skills can be used in a spirit of true listening, and all of them can be used in a rote, mechanical fashion. What makes the difference? What is true listening?

A STORY OF LISTENING FROM THE BIBLE

An incident in Mark 5:21-43 illustrates several aspects of good listening. Jesus had just returned from the other side of the Sea of Galilee and was approached by one of the leaders of the synagogue whose daughter was at the point of death. Jesus immediately set off with the synagogue leader.

They were followed by a large crowd, which included a desperate woman who had been bleeding for twelve years. "She had endured much under many physicians, and had spent all that she had; and she was no better, but rather grew worse" (verse 26). She thought that perhaps Jesus could heal her, so she jostled her way up to him and touched his cloak. She reasoned that if he was a true healer, touching his clothing would be enough.

She was right. She was immediately healed, but something happened that she had not expected. Jesus realized that power had gone out from him, so he stopped and looked around in the crowd, asking who touched his clothes. His disciples thought this was a very odd question. With such a huge crowd, of course many people had touched his clothes.

The woman knew that he was talking about her. She came and fell at his feet. Then she "told him the whole truth" (verse 33).

The synagogue leader's daughter was critically ill and close to death, and Jesus was on his way to heal her. He was busy with something important, and yet he stopped to listen to "the whole truth." If you've ever listened to someone talk about twelve years of medical adventures under the hands of numerous physicians, you know that "the whole truth" usually involves much emotion and countless details. The "whole truth" takes a while to tell. Yet Jesus stayed and paid attention until she was finished.

Perhaps the "whole truth" took three minutes to tell. Perhaps it took thirty minutes. However many minutes Jesus listened to the woman, his patience was remarkable. He was on his way to heal a child who was dying, after all.

I find it incredibly hard to listen when I'm in the middle of a task. I'm sure that's part of why I admire Jesus so much in this incident. I also find it hard to listen to one person when another person is pressuring me to deal with something else. Jesus' ability to focus on the woman and receive her whole story, while the synagogue leader was tugging on his sleeve either physically or metaphorically, provides a beautiful model of the significance of listening.

REALITY CHECK

I find it easy to talk a lot when I get wound up about a subject, so sometimes when my husband, Dave, and I have been with some other people, I ask him to give me feedback on my talking and listening. I'll say something like, "There were four of us, and I think I talked about a quarter of the time. Do you think I did?" Sometimes Dave's perception of what happened is similar to mine, and sometimes it's humiliatingly different.

For those of us who like to talk, the true and humbling fact about listening is that we have to shut up. When we are talking, we are not listening. Self-delusion about our ability to listen is all too common. In some cases we get so excited about something we can't slow down enough to focus on another person's concerns. Other times our own emotional needs are so great that we can't let in other people's concerns.

Sometimes I'll ask Dave for feedback about conversations I've had with him. "Did you feel listened to?" Sometimes he'll say yes and give me specific positive feedback: "You asked some good questions to draw me out." "You listened to my emotions." Other times he'll tell me that I seemed to want to give him advice or I seemed impatient with how he was feeling. I can do my job of shutting up in an attempt to listen, but if streams of advice are boiling inside my head or if I'm having strong judgmental thoughts about the other person's feelings, my listening will lack depth and quality.

Poor listening can come from other issues. Sometimes we are afraid that asking questions will seem invasive. Sometimes we don't know the basic skills of asking questions.

Carolyn, a medical transcriptionist in her forties, talked about the impact of personality type on listening:

> I was fairly introverted as a young person, and the one piece
> of advice that my mother gave me about making friends was

to be a good listener and let people know you're interested in them. It's the old standby, but it's true.

My son is away at college for the first time and is quite introverted. He recently told me he was very down because he felt he wasn't making any friends. I ended up giving him the same advice my mother gave me. I told him that before he can even listen to someone he would have to get beyond the "hi, hi" stage. In other words, after you say "hi" to someone and they say "hi" back, you can't let it die. I told him he has to continue on with another sentence that lets that person know you are really interested in them, something like, "How was your weekend?" or "How are your classes going?"

It seems so basic, but sometimes for someone who is introverted it just doesn't come naturally and has to be practiced. So he called me a couple of days after he went back to school and said he had done what I said and he was able to have a few conversations with people, and he was feeling much better. Now it's about three weeks later, and he has been doing a few things around campus with some of the new people he's getting to know. I know it's a struggle for him, but at least he's feeling better about himself.

I have tried to help him understand that he is who he is, that God made him who he is and everything that God creates is good, but he will have to work harder than some people at learning to feel comfortable meeting new people and making friends. It's hard as a mom to watch your kids struggle with making friends. But it was good to hear from him that he's making progress and slowly building some new relationships.

A few months later Carolyn told me, with delight, that her son had continued to practice listening and had made some friends.

Introversion and extroversion impact listening patterns in complex ways. Some introverts may be reluctant to invite someone's self-disclosure out of a fear of being overwhelmed by particularly intense sharing; or perhaps they've had bad experiences of welcoming self-disclosure, only to find themselves being colonized—their thoughts and emotions occupied, taken over and dominated—by someone with a particularly forceful personality. Of course, introverts may sometimes take refuge in listening, allowing someone's lengthy self-disclosing in order to avoid their own self-disclosure.

On the flip side, some extroverts might be listening as their own attempt at colonization, for example, the information hoarder who likes to size up and deconstruct other people, or the promiscuous listener who wants to be seen by others as "good to talk to." Or they may simply not be aware of the one-sidedness of the relationship they're cultivating, simply feeding their "curiosity about people" without actually committing anything to them.

LOVE MAKES THE DIFFERENCE

Deep listening comes from a willingness to let the other person be at the center of attention. Listening is entering into other people's worlds, letting them have the platform until they're finished. It's not about collecting factoids about other people or hoarding information. It's not about colonizing or being in control. It's not about using listening skills as a way to show we're great listeners, while feeling contemptuous and superior that someone would say such stupid things.

True listening, in fact, depends on having some measure of love for the person to whom we're listening. Listening as an act of friendship is a matter of quality.

"Love is patient." Love lets another person finish the topic they're talking about without turning the focus of the conversation back to ourselves. "Love is kind." Love serves the other person by entering into her or his feelings and thoughts. "Love is not envious or boastful or arrogant or rude. It does not rejoice in wrongdoing, but rejoices in the truth." Love is genuinely happy that a friend has experienced success at something that we would like to be successful at, and love is genuinely sad—with no gloating or second guessing—when our friend suffers.

First Corinthians 13:4-6, quoted in the previous paragraph, lays out the characteristics that separate good listeners from bad. Bad listeners are impatient. They seem anxious to get the conversation back onto their own life or interests. They don't exhibit kindness; they don't express empathy for what others are going through. They don't use those nonverbal or verbal messages that indicate concern for the other person's life. Bad listeners often seem to be boasting. They seem to need to talk about how they are better than others or know more. Sometimes bad listeners are flat-out rude, snatching conversations back to focus on themselves when others are still in the middle of a topic, ignoring significant concerns expressed by others.

In Colossians 3:12, the apostle Paul uses the metaphor of clothing to evoke the kind of behavior that he wants to see in the Christian community. His words are relevant when we consider the significance of careful listening: "As God's chosen ones, holy and beloved, clothe yourselves with compassion, kindness, humility, meekness, and patience." The five characteristics listed in this verse are excellent ways to describe a good listener. Putting them on like clothing, in those moments when we want to listen carefully to a friend, is exactly the right thing to do. We will be able to do that most effectively when we rest in God's love ourselves and realize that we are chosen and beloved of God.

"Above all, clothe yourselves with love, which binds everything together in perfect harmony" (Colossians 3:14). When I think of harmony, I think of the kind of peaceful quietness that removes my own tensions and anxieties so I can focus on another person's concerns. And harmony makes me think of music, which requires attentive listening and brings deep joy. The kind of love that results in careful listening brings joy because we know we are mirroring Christ's ability to enter into human life with interest and compassion.

We can seldom listen 100 percent along the lines of 1 Corinthians 13 and Colossians 3. Unpleasant thoughts will flit through our minds. "What a stupid thing to do," we might find ourselves thinking when another person describes something they did. "I could have handled that situation much better than my friend did." Or "I'm glad I'm not neurotic like that." We'll become impatient with the number of details or the over-the-top emotions we're hearing. We'll be tempted to take the conversation back and refocus it on ourselves. In fact, all too often we won't just be tempted to do it, we'll grab that conversation right back into our own hands and dive into our own story.

But we can try to listen. We can try to grow in our ability to listen. We can employ listening skills even when they feel artificial, asking God to help those skills to move from our mouths and our bodies into our hearts.

What does "listening" look like when I'm reading an online status update, an email or a blog post written by a friend? Or when I'm reading a text message on my cell phone? What do compassion, kindness, humility, meekness and patience look like when friends are across town or on the other side of the world, but we are reading words they have written?

Listening in electronic communication means slowing down enough to let our friend's words move from our minds to our hearts. Then we can figure out the best way to respond. The best response might involve using the same kind of communication or moving to another. Love means avoiding flippant, glib, self-aggrandizing comments, but love means more than that.

A brief response is usually better than nothing: "I got your email. Thanks. Hope to answer soon." With emails, I feel listened to when friends comment on what I said when I wrote to them. I feel listened to when friends post responses to my Facebook status updates. I particularly like responses that engage with the content or the issues I have raised. That engagement indicates listening.

One of my pet peeves is when people consistently answer my

emails without responding to a single thing I said when I wrote to them. Someone told me about having a colleague who doesn't feel listened to when close friends engage with one idea in an email but not all of them. In fact, some people plant "Easter eggs" in their written communication to see if people will pick up on their cues and ask them to elaborate.

REMEMBERING

One of the results of careful listening—whether that listening happens face-to-face or online—is that we are able to remember what is going on in a friend's life. Remembering enables us to follow up appropriately. "Last time we talked, you said you were just beginning a big project at work. Are you still in the middle of it, or is it finished? How did it go?" "In a Facebook post about a month ago, you mentioned your son was sick. How is he now?" "Your blog post about your trip to China was wonderful. Did you get over jet lag?"

Remembering enables us to ask whether the visit with a relative proved to be satisfying. Remembering helps us follow up with questions about the doctor's visit our friend was worried about, the exam she was facing or the big gardening project he was undertaking.

Some of that follow-up can happen in spontaneous encounters. Perhaps we run into a neighbor at the grocery store or a colleague in the mailroom. If we remember the specifics of what they were concerned about the last time we talked, we can follow up with a question that indicates our interest in the outcome.

Sometimes the follow-up requires intentional effort, such as a phone call, a text, an email or a purposeful walk across the street. Careful listening, resulting in remembering, can help bring to mind the person and his or her concerns. The appropriate response to remembering might involve making the effort to ask the person what happened. Careful listening, resulting in remembering, can help us understand the best way to engage in follow-up, whether to give a gift, an invitation to talk or a helpful action.

For many people, online communication plays a role in remembering. The photos on our friends' Facebook or Flickr pages remind us of their big fiftieth birthday party, their mission trip to Haiti, their child's graduation from elementary school, their obsession with baseball or their home remodel. Their online comments remind us of their love for birdwatching or biking.

These memory triggers help us stay up to date with the details of our friends' lives, so when we reconnect with them, we can focus on deeper issues. They help us pray for our friends' concerns. Paying attention to our friends' electronic communication can be a healthy form of listening, enabling us to express care and concern appropriately.

On the negative side, these electronic posts, so often superficial and trivial, can sidetrack us from deep connections with our friends. They can encourage us to focus on inconsequential matters in our friends' lives rather than their inner self. Looking behind the surface communications from friends, focusing on their heart values and deepest passions, requires great intentionality and careful listening even when we can see and listen to our friends face-to-face. Going deep requires even more intentionality and careful listening when the majority of our communication with them is electronic.

PRAYING

Listening and remembering are closely connected to prayer. When I listen carefully to a friend, I am more likely to know the best ways to pray about the situation she or he is concerned about. When I pray about something, it cements that person and that concern in my heart and mind, so I am more likely to remember it. Then I am more likely to reach out to the person and follow up in some way.

When I've prayed for friends, I'm more likely to be willing to listen the next time I have contact with them, because praying for something gives a level of investment in the outcome. I'll want to hear what happened after I prayed, so I'll be motivated to listen. And when I see the person a second time and ask about the concern, his or her situation is further bonded into my memory. Then I'm more likely to pray about it further.

Social Networking Across the Generations

About a year ago, Morgan, a researcher in his sixties, was surprised to see that a young adult from his congregation had friended him on Facebook. Morgan said yes to the request, and in the next few weeks several other people in their late teens and twenties from church friended him on Facebook as well.

Morgan comments on Facebook posts by the young adults, often with just a few words and often with humor. In one case, a young man was dealing with custody issues for his two children. Morgan responded to this man's Facebook posts with words of support and told the man that he was praying for him.

On Sundays, Morgan seldom talks with the young adults with whom he is connected online. They are too busy talking with their age mates. They may wave at Morgan or smile across the room, but the majority of their communication with him happens online, and most of the online conversation isn't particularly profound. The value, Morgan believes, is "that I have contact with them at all, on whatever level, from the trivial to the serious. It's being *visible* in their lives, I guess." Morgan is engaging in a form of listening that conveys his respect for the young adults at his church.

As friends, how can we learn to listen and remember better? One way is to pray for our friends consistently.

This ebb and flow between listening and prayer is particularly significant when a friend or acquaintance experiences some kind of crisis. Nothing embarrasses me more than to forget something important that a friend has told me about. I can remember all too many times when I have run into a friend and blithely said, "How are you doing?" They answer back by telling me about the cancer, job loss or family death that we talked about the last time we met. I try to mask the fact that I had totally forgotten about that situation. I don't want to hurt the person I'm talking to. Even if I do succeed in covering up my lack of memory, I feel ashamed that I have missed an opportunity to pray for that friend's need. I have violated the heart of friendship.

Over and over in my interviews, people told me that a key attribute of friendship is sticking with someone in crisis, being available when needed, responding with practical help or a listening ear when times are tough. Friendship involves being faithful and caring in the challenges of life.

PRAYING TO A HIKOI GOD

Nelson, a retired minister in his seventies, was diagnosed with lung cancer about a year ago. He and his wife decided to tell only a few of their friends, the people he would call "soul friends." He described the friends they chose to tell: "All are Christian but come from very different positions, some on the edge of church life and some deeply involved. All of them are given to prayer and meditation. What became obvious very quickly was their faithfulness. They held me daily, and I knew it. I could feel a kind of surrounding."

Maori are the indigenous people of New Zealand, and one of these friends had strong connections with the Maori tradition and heritage. This friend began what he called a "hikoi." *Hikoi* is a Maori word that refers to a ceremonial walk, a parade or a protest walk. Numerous political and religious marches in New Zealand have been referred to as hikoi.

This man's hikoi consisted of an hour-long vigil every Monday and Thursday night for Nelson. He used the Bible readings for the day from the lectionary, and he meditated on those Scriptures and prayed for Nelson.

The best part for Nelson was what happened on Tuesdays and Fridays. "I would get an email the next day which held his thoughts and a prayer to the 'hikoi God' for me and my wife on our journey. So far there have been eighty-four messages. His faithfulness is a thing of great beauty and promise."

Nelson reported, "The hikoi has now changed direction. One of the friends has also developed lymph cancer and is facing chemotherapy. We will hold him with the same faithfulness."

The ceremonial walk or protest march evoked by the word *hikoi* conveys profound truths about the nature of the listening, remembering and praying that provides support to friends in need. Indeed, when we enter into a friend's illness or other crisis, we are protesting against that awful thing they are facing. We are ceremonially walking with them, and our listening, remembering and praying fit into an ancient pattern of journeying with people in crisis. Friends throughout the centuries have cared for the ones they love who are experiencing difficulties. Friends throughout the centuries have prayed and offered timeless forms of help and support.

I've read so many articles asserting that online relationships are inferior to face-to-face relationships. What the writers of those articles ignore is that almost all relationships these days have an online or electronic component. The hikoi for Nelson was an enormous gift to him. Nothing can replace that kind of prayer, faithfulness and devotion to a friend's needs. But notice that Nelson's friend used email to send updates to him.

For most of my interviewees, text messages, email, online social networking and Skype function as tools that serve real and meaningful relationships. They can be overused, and they can become addictive, and these are significant challenges that must be frequently assessed. But because electronic communication is embedded in everyday life for most people, we need to consider what it looks like to be a faithful friend in our world today, a world where new forms of communication play a role in so many things we do. A face-to-face conversation or a long, thoughtful email or letter can give us depth of information, which is wonderful to have. But with intentionality, even brief mentions of concerns, conveyed to us by electronic forms of communication, can reveal a lot about how to pray for a friend.

The kind of remembering that nurtures friendships can occur in person or through electronic communication. The teenagers and young adults I interviewed use frequent text messages to follow up with friends. "How did the exam go?" "How was the party you were so nervous about?" "Did you get the job?" "Is your difficult workmate bothering you today?" All of those brief questions show that we have remembered what matters to our friend. Those questions show support.

Kirsten, forty, often texts her friends with urgent prayer requests. I often pray for things I read on my friends' Facebook status updates, and I often check up by email with friends to ask about challenges that I remember they're facing. My husband Skypes regularly with our older son, asking him about the small and large crises of his life.

A key friendship skill for our time, expressed by many in my interviews, involves knowing what form of communication will serve a friend in the best way. When we read a brief text message or online status update about a recent cancer diagnosis or a death in the family, that brief news item should usually precipitate a switch in the form of communication to something more personal, perhaps an email, phone call or visit, so that appropriate concern can be expressed.

Listening, remembering and praying—in response to information received through any means of communication—lay the foundation for actions that show love and support to friends. If I'm paying attention to what's happening in my friend's life through whatever means I receive that information, I'll be more likely to be able to give the right gift or provide practical help in the best way.

Am I listening to, remembering and praying for my friends with perseverance, commitment and love? Or am I frittering away opportunities to show love?

QUESTIONS FOR REFLECTION, JOURNALING, DISCUSSION OR ACTION

- Who are the people who have listened to you deeply and carefully? What words, sounds or actions do they use to indicate that they are listening? In what ways have you or could you learn from their example?

- Who are the people who frustrate you because they don't listen well? How do you feel when you're with them? What characteristics and actions indicate that they aren't listening?

- What helps you remember the emotions and needs your friends express, so you can follow up later? In what ways would you like to do a better job in remembering? What might help you remember better?

- What helps you remember how to pray for your friends? In what ways would you like to pray more consistently for your friends? What might help you do that?

- This week, monitor your own listening patterns. Try to observe what you do well as a listener and where you need to grow. Watch for those moments when listening seems particularly difficult, and try to figure out what's going on inside you that makes it hard to focus on the other person and let her or him have the floor.

- Spend some time praying about the role of listening in the way you practice friendship. Ask God for insight to understand why you do what you do, and ask God for help to grow as a listener.

9

ASKING · GIVING · THANKING

Our real friends are the people we have spent time with, shared experiences with, told our secrets to, exchanged ideas with, supported through difficult times or allowed to support us.
—Hope, an office manager in her forties

Friendship is a commitment to a relationship with another person that involves being intentional about working on the best possible communication with each other and understanding how to serve each other.
—Emma, a project manager in her fifties

Daniel, in his sixties, was raised with the notion that men are supposed to be independent and strong, able to meet their own needs. He joked that the Simon and Garfunkel song "I Am a Rock" summarizes the philosophy of manhood he learned as a child. The stoicism encouraged for men spilled over to all of his family life. Even his mother was afraid to acknowledge weaknesses or needs. The shame of needing someone's help was very strong.

People have told Daniel that asking others for help can be a way to build intimacy. He has found it difficult to act on that idea, but he has tried. He can see that the extreme self-reliance of his parents wasn't good for them or for their children, because it resulted in isolation and alienation from neighbors and family members.

Daniel volunteers with an international student ministry at the local university. The small group of students decided they would like to hold a retreat over spring break. As Daniel was praying about the possibility of holding a retreat, he remembered that a couple he knew from his church had a holiday cottage. He wondered if perhaps they might be willing to loan the cottage to the student group for the retreat.

He didn't know the couple well, but he got up the courage to ask about the cottage. They were enthusiastic about the idea, and asked Daniel and his wife to meet them at the cottage for lunch a couple of weeks later.

The lunch was fun, and Daniel got a good preview of the cottage so he could begin to make plans for the retreat. As the retreat drew nearer, Daniel consulted with the couple about some of the plans, and after the retreat he was able to share with them some of the good things that happened. All those conversations about the retreat drew Daniel closer to the couple. Asking for help had indeed increased intimacy and set him on a path toward friendship with them.

ASKING

Friends ask for all sorts of things: help with projects, a listening ear when times are tough, prayer support in the midst of challenges, companionship in activities, a few moments to brainstorm possible solutions to a problem, and many other things. The give-and-take of asking and receiving is an integral part of friendship.

Why is asking so hard for so many people? I have observed that the most isolated people often have a hard time asking for help. Daniel's story illustrates the impact of the "rock and island" philosophy of being a man. "What's wrong with you that you can't figure it out on your own?" These words float around in his head when he considers asking for help. The pride of being self-sufficient is a strong motivator for many men, and it influences many women as well.

In fact, Daniel's mother experienced as much, if not more, shame than Daniel's father when she had needs. She found it excruciatingly difficult to ask for help or acknowledge a weakness.

She experienced a major health crisis without telling her family members. When they found out about it many years later, they were stunned that she had not been able to ask for support and encouragement in the midst of a medical challenge that could not possibly have been considered to be her fault. She died a lonely, isolated woman. Her inability to acknowledge her need for help played a significant role in her isolation.

Pride in self-sufficiency and shame in asking for help are two major forces that make it difficult to admit we have needs. In addition, we may fear that our friends are too busy to help or have too many struggles of their own. We don't want to impose on people who are already stretched. We don't want to be a burden.

JEREMIAH AND BARUCH

The story of Jeremiah and Baruch illustrates the relationship between asking and intimacy. Jeremiah, that passionate and beleaguered prophet in the Bible, got lots of help from a man named Baruch. Jeremiah 32 describes an incident when God told Jeremiah to buy a field as an act of hope for the future of Israel. Jeremiah asked Baruch to bury the deed for the field in a clay jar so it would be safe for the future, and Baruch obeyed Jeremiah's request.

Jeremiah 36 records more. God instructed Jeremiah to write down the words God had given him, so Jeremiah again solicited help from Baruch. Jeremiah dictated God's words to Baruch, and Baruch wrote them on a scroll. Jeremiah had been banned from the temple, so he asked Baruch to take the scroll to the temple and read it out loud. Ultimately the news about this scroll came to the king, who chopped it into pieces and burned it in his coal fire, a dramatic portrayal of someone who passionately wanted to avoid hearing and obeying God. The king then set out to arrest Baruch and Jeremiah.

"But the Lord hid them" (Jeremiah 36:26), so they were safe. Then the Lord instructed Jeremiah to write down all the words of prophesy again, so once again Baruch recorded Jeremiah's words on a scroll.

Baruch is often called Jeremiah's secretary, and indeed he filled that role. But he did more. He entered into Jeremiah's call from God and helped him in more ways than simply writing down his words. He traveled with Jeremiah and shared Jeremiah's emotions (see Jeremiah 43:1-4; 45:1-5).

Jeremiah is one of my favorite books of the Bible, and I like to ponder the fact that we probably owe its existence to Baruch's willingness to write it down. Twice. Baruch's loyalty illustrates the kind of friendship that can exist between people who are willing to serve God and do as they are asked, even if the roles they have been given are very different.

Jeremiah asked for Baruch's help numerous times. Their friendship also illustrates the kind of partnership that develops when someone is willing to ask for help and someone else is willing to give it.

GIVING, ASKING, NOTICING AND THANKING

Giving in friendship can involve providing help in a variety of ways. Giving includes presents. In the broadest sense, all acts of kindness in friendship are gifts: listening carefully, sending a card or message expressing sympathy, or accepting that a friend is experiencing extraordinary challenges at work and won't be able to spend time together for a while. Acts of initiative can also be viewed as gifts of friendship: reaching out to someone who is new in town or new on the job, or sharing a vulnerable feeling with a friend to indicate he or she can do the same with you. Offering forgiveness after being hurt may be one of the biggest gifts a friend can give.

Misunderstandings in friendship can arise when two people give gifts to each other in different ways. One of them buys presents and the other tries to give the gift of practical help or a listening ear. A discussion of languages of love can be illuminating.

I have observed that people who have a rich circle of friends have learned the friendship skills of asking for help and giving a variety of gifts. They have also learned the significance of thanking the people who help them or give to them in any way. My understanding of the significance of asking for help in friendship has been influenced by my own growth in thankfulness.

For more than fifteen years I have been giving special focus to thankfulness in my prayers. That focus has forced me to pay more attention to the good gifts God has given me in daily life. Noticing what God is giving me has spilled over to noticing what people are giving me. Noticing, and then expressing thanks, are great intimacy builders, both with God and with friends.

David Steindl-Rast, a Benedictine monk, wrote a book on thankfulness in prayer that lays out the way that giving and thanking build intimacy. In *Gratefulness, the Heart of Prayer,* he writes,

> Why is it so difficult to acknowledge a gift as a gift? Here is the reason. When I admit that something is a gift, I admit my dependence on the giver. This may not sound that difficult, but there is something within us that bristles at the idea of dependence. . . . When I acknowledge a gift received, I acknowledge a bond that binds me to the giver.[1]

When we ask for help in any form, we are asking for someone to give us something. We're asking for a gift. Asking for a gift implies that we are depending on the giver, that we are dependent people. Thanking the person for the gift reinforces that dependence. When we thank the giver for that gift, we acknowledge the bond between us. Bonds between people are a form of dependence, and acknowledging our need for those kinds of bonds requires that we relinquish at least some of our pride in our own self-sufficiency.

Daniel's mother couldn't face the idea that she might be dependent on another person, so she couldn't ask for help. She missed out on the bond that forms between people when they give gifts to each other and express gratitude to each other.

Steindl-Rast believes that this bond that develops between giver and thanksgiver helps us understand the significance of gratitude in prayer. I have discovered his words to be true as I have grown in willingness to engage in prayers of thankfulness. Prayers of thankfulness acknowledge our dependence on God. Taking the time to notice all the ways God has blessed us and cared for us nurtures our relationship with God, because with each prayer of thankfulness we acknowledge that we need God.

WE BELONG TOGETHER

In the same way, giving and thanking shape friendships. When we ask for help, we are giving our friend a gift, the opportunity to give a gift back to us. And when we thank our friend for that gift, we acknowledge we depend on our friend. We need our friend, and we honestly admit that need. And this binds us together.

Steindl-Rast believes that the person "who says 'thank you' to another really says, 'we belong together.' Giver and thanksgiver belong together."[2] When we ask for help, we create a situation in which we affirm that we belong together with the person we are asking for help. When we thank that person, we are continuing to affirm that we are connected.

I have found that asking for small favors is a great way to nurture a fledgling friendship. Living in a new country and new city, I have found myself asking all sorts of small questions: "Can you help me understand how the city council works here?" "Can you tell me which restaurants you like?" "Where do you buy gardening tools?" Later, when I act on the answers to those questions, I feel grateful to the people who gave me the information, and I try to remember to thank them.

Question asking in online settings builds intimacy in the same small way. "Does anyone know a motel near the Los Angeles airport?" Later, thanking the person who provided the name of a motel affirms the connection between giver and receiver.

Even though I am thousands of miles from my closest friends, I continue to ask for their help. Using email, I ask for advice, prayer support and sometimes practical help with something I can't do from a distance. And then I thank them.

The significance of thankfulness in friendship cannot be over-estimated. Perhaps gushing expressions of thanks can be over-done, but noticing the many ways the people around us contribute to our lives, and trying to thank them appropriately, is a key friendship skill.

I have watched my mother write hundreds, perhaps thousands, of thank-you notes. She adheres to an old standard of etiquette. Every time she has a meal at another person's house, every time she attends a party and every time she receives a gift of any kind, she writes a thank-you note. I don't write anywhere near as many thank-you notes as she does, but I make a concerted effort to notice all the ways the people around me are helping me. I try to thank them through a personal word of thanks in a conversation, a thank-you by email or other online means or sometimes a thank-you note.

Friends help us in so many ways, even when we haven't asked for help. "Thanks for listening to me ramble on about my job the other day. It was helpful to get it out." "Thanks for the lunch we had last week. I enjoyed the conversation." "Thanks for giving me a lift to the meeting on Thursday. It was great not to have to drive." "Thanks for photocopying that article you thought I would enjoy. I appreciate that you remembered me." "Thanks for your email. I loved hearing from you."

OBSTACLES TO THANKFULNESS IN FRIENDSHIP

Perhaps we are slow to thank people because we really don't want to admit that we need others. We don't want to admit that kind of weakness. Perhaps we don't express thanks because we are so caught up in the stresses of our lives that we forget to take the time for that note or word of thanks. Perhaps we are so caught up in our own lives that we forget to notice what other people have done for us. We can't thank people for something we haven't taken the time to notice.

Perhaps the consumer culture has influenced us in deep and profound ways, encouraging us to focus our attention on what we don't have, rather than noticing what we do have. The sea of advertisements that washes over us encourages us to believe that we need something more. The consumer culture tells us that what we have is not enough. Buy, buy, buy. Whatever you have is inadequate; you need more. If we are experiencing abundance, if we are feeling happy with life, we'll quit shopping.

In this sea of advertising, noticing the great gifts God has given us requires intentionality and effort. In the same way, paying attention to what our friends have given us requires a shift of focus away from what we lack. Thankfulness is rooted in noticing what we have been given.

The Colossians 3 passage cited throughout this book places a strong emphasis on thankfulness. Paul instructs,

> And let the peace of Christ rule in your hearts, to which indeed you were called in the one body. And be thankful. Let the word of Christ dwell in you richly; teach and admonish one another in all wisdom; and with gratitude in your hearts sing psalms, hymns, and spiritual songs to God. And whatever you do, in word or deed, do everything in the name of the Lord Jesus, giving thanks to God the Father through him. (Colossians 3:15-17)

Thankfulness and gratitude are mentioned three times in those three verses. Gratitude toward God is stressed, but gratitude toward others is implied. Thankfulness enables us to live more fully in peace, because thankfulness admits that we need God and we need others, which is the honest truth. The pride of self-sufficiency reduces peace, because it is fundamentally dishonest about who we are as human beings. Thankfulness for the caring actions of the people around us affirms that we were created to live in relationship.

Thankfulness shapes us because we take the time to notice the ways people are contributing to our lives. Thankfulness builds bridges because giver and thanksgiver acknowledge their dependence on each other.

Friends ask each other for help and companionship. Friends thank each other for all the ways the friendship nourishes them. Asking, giving, receiving and thanking create bonds between people that say, "We belong together."

QUESTIONS FOR REFLECTION, JOURNALING, DISCUSSION OR ACTION

- In what situations or with which friends do you find it difficult to ask for help or companionship? In which situations or with which friends do you find it easier to ask for help or companionship?

- Ponder the obstacles you experience in asking for help from friends. Are they rooted in models of relationships from your family of origin or other childhood influences? Are they rooted in pride in self-sufficiency or shame in having needs? In what ways would you like to respond to these obstacles?

- In what ways do you like to give to your friends? Time? Gifts? Words? Helpful actions? Explore the reasons why you like to give in that way.

- Do you find it easy or hard to thank people? Have you experienced someone else's thanks as a step closer in intimacy with them? Why or why not?

- This week, ask two or three of your friends, colleagues or acquaintances how they would define *friend* or *friendship*. Watch particularly for any components of their definition that relate to asking, giving, receiving and thanking.

- Spend time praying about your patterns of asking, giving, receiving and thanking. Ask God for insight to understand why you do what you do, and ask God for help to grow in these areas.

10

SHARING · CARING · BEING TOGETHER · BEING APART

Many friendships grow out of need—young mothers, neighbors, colleagues. Others grow out of interests—golf, Bible study, writers' and political groups. Some just grow out of proximity. In all these networks, many connections do not grow into significant friendships. But some do.
—Maria, a teacher in her sixties

A friendship is a deep and meaningful relationship, important to both of us. We do not have to have constant contact, but when needed, I can call on this person in a heartbeat.
—Julia, a social worker in her forties

When I was twenty-one, I read *The Four Loves* by C. S. Lewis. His views influenced my understanding of friendship for many years. Lewis's description of friendship love evokes the metaphor of two people standing shoulder to shoulder. Perhaps the two friends both enjoy collecting antiques or going to movies or playing soccer. They become connected to each other because of that shared interest, and the shared interest is the focus of their attention. So, in effect, they are standing beside each other, shoulder to shoulder, looking at that shared interest.[1]

Lewis contrasted friendship love with romantic love, in which the two people are focused on each other. Instead of standing shoulder to shoulder, looking at their shared interest, romantic love motivates us to face the other person, looking into his or her eyes, enjoying that person for exactly who he or she is.

For many years I tried to fit my relationships into the pattern described by Lewis. It worked to some extent. As a twenty-something adult, many of my friendships focused on common interests such as reading, music, traveling, exercising and so on. To some extent, my friends and I did stand shoulder to shoulder, looking at the things in which we shared an interest. In my twenties, I fell in love and got married, and much of my new relationship with my new husband involved facing toward each other, learning to enjoy each other for who we really are.

Then we had children. My husband and I became partners in parenthood, standing shoulder to shoulder to raise our children, while trying to retain those moments of facing one another to keep romantic love kindled.

During my late twenties and early thirties, most of my friends were also young moms. Much of our time involved the shared interest of parenting. But I began to realize that what I long for in friendships is not simply shared interests. I also want to be appreciated for who I am, and I sense that most of my friends want that as well.

I looked back on the childhood friendship that was most significant and transformative for me, my friendship with Wendy, and I realized that two components were present in our friendship: we shared interests in many things, but we also appreciated each other. At times as teenagers we stood shoulder to shoulder, looking at—or experiencing together—books, rock music, boys, clothes, skiing and a myriad of other things. Sometimes we talked about how we thought and felt about things, and an aspect of those conversations involved facing each other and expressing our enjoyment for the way the other person was made. We gave each other gifts and compliments that were designed to affirm that we knew and loved each other for who we were.

With the young moms who had become my friends, we did the

Jonathan and David: Loyalty and Intimacy

David and Jonathan, more than any pair of friends in the Bible, have been immortalized in articles, books, plays, movies and even operas. Their friendship is described in 1 Samuel 18–20. The two men swore an oath of faithfulness to each other. Some translations of 1 Samuel 20:17 say that Jonathan loved David "as he loved his own life" (for example, NRSV), while others say "he loved him as he loved his own soul" (for example, ASV).

Jonathan and David have always been models of what I call "soul friends," deep, faithful, intimate friends. I admire Jonathan's loyalty to David. Jonathan was the oldest son of King Saul and probably expected to be king of Israel someday. But when God made clear that David would be the next king, Jonathan remained loyal to David and even jeopardized his own life to protect him.

Friends throughout the ages have been comforted and challenged by the level of intimacy and support Jonathan and David gave to each other. Jewish writers in the Mishnah, as well as some of the early church fathers, believed that their friendship is an example to us because they model the kind of love that is given without expectation of reward.

same thing. Sometimes we went on outings with our children or talked about the tasks of motherhood. Other times we faced each other and truly listened to each other's thoughts and feelings about life and faith, and through that listening and our words in response, we communicated our care for and acceptance of the other.

FRIENDSHIP DIALECTICS

Numerous scholars have built on a 1992 book by William K. Rawlins called *Friendship Matters*,[2] and Rawlins and those other scholars use the word *dialectic* to describe several tensions that exist within friendships. This pattern I have been describing fits into the dialectic they call "affection versus instrumentality."

Affection in a friendship relates to all those ways we express our care for another person, the gifts, words, touch, actions and listening that show we care for someone else. When we are expressing affection we are, in effect, standing face-to-face with our friend. We are paying attention to the specific ways we can connect emotionally, and perhaps spiritually, with that friend.

Instrumentality in a friendship relates to all the ways a friendship fulfills a function, all those ways friends stand shoulder to shoulder, looking at or engaging with something. Jon and Colin play racquetball every Friday after work. Sarah and Janet get together on Tuesday morning to quilt. Friends meet on the soccer field to kick a ball around, at the local pool so their kids can learn to swim and at the church on Wednesday mornings at six to study the Bible. Friends do things together that can't be done alone, or they do things together that are more fun to do with someone else. Friends help each other out. Many friendships have a functional aspect, which Rawlins describes as instrumental. The friendship is an instrument to meet a goal.

All friendships have to navigate this tension between affection and instrumentality. Friends have to decide how much they will engage in a friendship that meets a functional need, the instrumental aspect of friendship, and how much they will express affection in a friendship. Most friendships move naturally between the two ends of the spectrum.

I met one of my closest friends when we both had teenaged sons, and we supported each other through the challenges of parenting teens. We brainstormed ways of coping with our sons, and we prayed for each other. We also listened to each other's emotions and affirmed each other in those difficult years. Our friendship had aspects that involved both function and affection. For us, the affection has been constant, and the functional aspects of the friendship have shifted over the years.

When my husband and I moved away from Seattle and we rented out our house, my friend acted as our agent in managing the rental. Then we sold the house, and my friend and I now have fewer functional aspects to our friendship. But we still pray for each other in the challenges of our lives, communicating by email and phone. Prayer communicates affection, but it also has a functional aspect in a friendship.

Being aware of this tension between instrumentality and affection can be helpful in keeping a friendship rich, alive and growing. Jon and Colin, who play racquetball together each week, have found that every few weeks or so they need to have a conversation as well as engage in the sport together. When they neglect to connect personally because they are so focused on fitness, they experience increasing irritation with each other, and their friendship seems to flounder.

The classic thank-you note, thank-you gift or other expression of thanks helps to navigate this tension. When a friend does something functional above and beyond the normal pattern of the friendship—prepared several meals because someone in the family is sick, taken photographs at a birthday party, helped out with an onerous gardening project—the friendship has moved in the direction of instrumentality. A warm and caring thank-you—verbal, written or in the form of a gift—helps move the friendship back in the direction of affection, because it expresses how valuable the other person is.

William Rawlins believed that a friendship with a strong component of affection will be stronger than a friendship focused primarily on function (instrumentality). I know I look for affection, first and foremost, in my friendships, and the definitions of friendship throughout this book have a strong affection component. However, C. S. Lewis reminds us that shared interests can function as a foundation for friendship. In many cases, we meet people first through shared interests, on a soccer team, in a quilting group, at an art society or in a book club. Many of the contacts we make in the workplace originate in the shared interest of getting the job done.

Some of the people we meet through shared interests will become friends. Our affection for them will complement the functional aspect of the relationship, and some degree of friendship will develop.

PAUL AND BARNABAS: INSTRUMENTALITY AND AFFECTION

Many of the biblical stories of friendship portray the interweaving of instrumentality and affection. The friendships between Jonathan and David, Ruth and Naomi, Jeremiah and Baruch, and Mary and Elizabeth had aspects of function and aspects of affection. I see those two components in the joint ministry of Paul and Barnabas, described in Acts 13–15. They traveled together, preaching the gospel and ministering to Christians. There can be no doubt, reading those three chapters, that their relationship had a strong functional aspect to it. In fact, Acts 13:2-3 describes the moment in a worship service in Antioch when the Holy Spirit spoke: "Set apart for me Barnabas and Saul for the work to which I have called them."

Their working relationship also had a strong component of affection. Barnabas's real name was Joseph, but the disciples chose to call him Barnabas, which means "son of encouragement" (Acts 4:36). His encouraging personality first becomes visible to the reader of Acts when Paul came to Jerusalem after meeting Jesus and becoming a Christian. The Christians in Jerusalem were afraid of Paul because he used to persecute them. They doubted that he was truly a Christian, so they wouldn't let him join them. Barnabas stepped in, bringing Paul into their midst. Barnabas "described for them how on the road he had seen the Lord, who had spoken to him, and how in Damascus he had spoken boldly in the name of Jesus" (Acts 9:27).

Barnabas was able to see past the surface of Paul's life. He could see who Paul really was and how he had changed. That ability to look deeply at another person is a characteristic of affection.

Acts 15:36-40 describes the disagreement that led to separate ministries for Paul and Barnabas. Because travel in the ancient world was so difficult and letters so rare, they may have had little contact for the rest of their lives. I often wonder what they thought about each other after the disagreement. We have a bit of evidence to indicate that their respect and affection endured. Paul mentions Barnabas cordially in 1 Corinthians 9:6 and Colossians 4:10. Both letters were written after the split, suggesting that Paul continued to think about Barnabas with gratitude and affection.

AFFECTION AND INSTRUMENTALITY ONLINE
These concepts have relevance in the online world. With the growing access to information, friendships online often fulfill the function of helping others sort through the growing mass of information.

My younger son has a blog. He posts photos of his trips and comments about own life. But much of his blog involves his thoughts about articles he has read. He posts links to book and movie reviews, articles about social trends and opinion pieces. He describes what he believes to be the significance of those articles.

Many of my Facebook friends post links to their own blogs or links to articles they have enjoyed. I'm not interested in spending a lot of time cruising around the Internet to find things to read, so I find the links on my son's blog and the links posted by my Facebook friends to be very helpful. They steer me to interesting information and stimulating ideas.

I notice that some of my Facebook friends post questions asking for specific information, and their friends provide answers to those questions. Does anyone know of a good restaurant in Atlanta? Has anyone dealt with warts? Can anyone help me think of places to take my mother when she visits next week? In chapter three you met Sam, a teenage break-dancer, who uses an online break-dancing forum to get news about events and to ask advice of other dancers. All these forms of sharing resources and specific information online are manifestations of the instrumental aspect of friendship. They fulfill a function.

Affection can be expressed online as well by commenting on people's photos, congratulating them on their achievements, thanking them for posting links and writing longer messages using traditional email or the email function on social-networking websites.

Part of why I enjoy Facebook so much is that I can respond to the updates, links and photos that people post. Facebook has a "like" button that I can quickly click if I want to let people know I enjoyed something they posted. If I want to say something more specific, Facebook lets me do that as well by commenting on thoughts and links my Facebook friends have posted. Those comments are public; anyone who is a friend of my friend and can see what they posted will also be able to see what I wrote in response. So when I comment on something someone has posted, I have to be aware that many people I don't know may read that comment. Facebook's email feature makes it possible to comment privately, and sometimes I do that.

All of these comments can be glib, joking, lighthearted responses that are fun and casual. But I see plenty of statements in comments by others that express affection and support. And I try to make sure that many of my own comments also express affection and affirmation.

Another of Rawlins's dialectics helps explain tensions that can arise in friendships. He proposes that all friends have to navigate the tension between independence and dependence as they decide how much time to spend together and how many interests and activities they will engage in with their friend versus without their friend.

THE DIALECTIC OF INDEPENDENCE
AND DEPENDENCE

My mother jokes about the year my father retired from his job. His retirement precipitated a shift in the balance in the amount of time my parents spent together and apart. Mom had a routine of volunteering, golfing, doing household tasks and running errands. My dad didn't want to volunteer or golf with her, and he wasn't too eager to take up new household tasks. But he did want to spend time with her.

"Where are you going?" he would ask when she picked up her purse to leave the house.

"To the grocery store."

"I'll just ride along with you."

In that first year after my father's retirement, Mom came to dread the words "I'll just ride along with you." His presence on errands slowed Mom, distracted her and made things more com-

Doing Nothing Together

I'm eighteen, my first time living away from home. I do the necessary studying, but I spend hours and hours hanging out with friends, "wasting" time. We talk, listen to music and take pictures of each other doing crazy things.

I'm twenty-two, working at my first job. My roommate, Maggie, and I spend hours and hours hanging out together, talking about every topic under the sun.

I'm twenty-four, recently married. My husband and I spend hours and hours hanging out together, just enjoying each other.

Luke 10:38-42 records an incident when Jesus visits the home of his friends. Martha is bustling around doing tasks, while Mary sits at Jesus' feet, listening to him. Jesus commends Mary for choosing the better path. Mary, Jesus affirms, was not "wasting" time.

That story calls us to spend time with Jesus. It also illustrates the value of simply being with friends. Does hanging out with a friend include having a long conversation by texting? A conversation by instant message or Facebook chat? Can it include poring over a friend's photos online and commenting on them? With the strong cultural emphasis on productivity, we need to rediscover and reaffirm the value of simply being with friends, and we need to reshape our understanding of all the options for what it can look like today.

plicated. After a year or two, my father had settled into his own rhythms, so the issue faded in significance. Their adjustment reflects this challenge that Rawlins has described as the dialectic of independence and dependence.

A healthy friendship involves the freedom to explore and engage in activities apart from each other, as well as the freedom to ask for help, support and companionship. With friends who are not particularly close, often the greatest challenge involves getting up the courage to ask for help, support or companionship. With friends who are very close, often the greatest challenge is to acknowledge the need for time away from that friend, time to do something independently.

Many events like retirement can change the pattern of dependence and independence in a friendship: a move, an illness, a job change, a marriage, the birth of a child, the empty nest. Many of these events precipitate unexpected changes.

A friend gets a new job and suddenly stops playing racquetball with you, something you had not foreseen, particularly because you had gone to a lot of effort to keep in contact with this friend after you got your new job, which is ten times more demanding than your old one. It hurts. Another friend gets married and disappears from the friendship circle. Two of your friends have babies. One of them suddenly spends much less time with you because of absorption with the baby, while the other decides to stay home after many years in a busy career. Suddenly she (or he) is posting dozens of photos online and calling and texting all the time, desiring companionship in a way that wasn't necessary with a full-time job.

Over time, friendships shift and change. Patterns of independence and dependence ebb and flow, as do patterns of instrumentality and affection. Being aware of these patterns helps us pay attention to what's happening in friendships. They can help us ask questions of our friends and learn about their concerns for the friendship. They can help us pray for our friendships.

In the next two chapters we'll consider issues that relate to

Rawlins's other dialectics in friendship. Those dialectics—the tension between the ideal and the real, between judgment and acceptance, and between expressiveness and protectiveness—often precipitate additional challenges and conflicts in friendships, and we'll explore the implications of those tensions.

QUESTIONS FOR REFLECTION, JOURNALING, DISCUSSION OR ACTION

• Spend time considering your closest friendships. Make a list of the most frequent activities you do with your friends. Which activities are functional (instrumental)? Which activities nurture affection between the two of you? Which activities do both? In your close friendships, do you desire to move more in the direction of affection or instrumentality?

• Spend time doing the same kind of analysis in the area of dependence and independence. In any of your friendships, do you feel pulled by your friends to be more dependent or independent than you desire? How have you handled that tension? How would you like to handle it?

• Have you noticed that either of these two dialectics—instrumentality versus affection or dependence versus independence—have precipitated conflict in your friendships? How have you navigated that conflict?

• This week, ask two or three more friends, colleagues or acquaintances how they would define *friendship*. Watch for aspects of their definition that connect with the ideas in this book. Watch particularly for any components of their definition that connect with the themes of instrumentality, affection, independence and dependence.

• Spend some time praying about your friendship patterns in the areas of instrumentality, affection, independence and dependence. Ask God for insight to understand why you do what you do, and ask for help to grow in these areas.

11

PACING · CHOOSING

A friend is someone with whom I have a reciprocal relationship, whom I know I can trust with a secret or confession even if I don't necessarily choose to confide deeply with them.
—Lewis, a photographer in his thirties

A friend is someone with whom you have an ongoing conversation. Even if there is a break in time between contacts, you can pick up the thread as if it were yesterday.
—Lydia, an accountant in her forties

My husband, Dave, and I were driving home after a wonderful evening with some new friends. "That was fun," Dave said enthusiastically. "I had a great time. Did you?"

"I did. I really enjoyed the conversation. They're so interesting to talk to."

"Let's invite them over for dinner soon."

"Yes, I definitely want to have them over. But not too soon."

Pacing in friendships matters. My mother modeled careful and intentional pacing in friendship, and her model has been very helpful to me. She seemed to have a mental calendar that sent messages to her conscious mind: *You haven't seen Susan for two months, and that's about how often you tend to see her, so it's time to make contact with her. You haven't seen Rebecca for three weeks, and that's longer than the usual spacing between your usual contacts with her. You prob-*

ably need to check and see what's going on with her. John and Rhonda have invited you to events four times in the past six months. That's much more often than in the past. What's going on there?

Friendships develop a rhythm, and part of the challenge of managing friendships involves discovering or establishing what that rhythm will be. When Dave and I had that enjoyable dinner with new friends, I wanted to consider the rhythm we might establish with them. I didn't want to invite them back for dinner two or three weeks later, because I knew we couldn't sustain a relationship with them that involved getting together every two or three weeks. Every two or three months might work, I thought, so I wanted to get the friendship into that rhythm from the beginning.

Rhythm and pacing in friendship, as in dancing, usually involve more than one person. I might meet someone I like, and I'd enjoy having lunch with that new friend every week or two. But that new friend might have a very different expectation. Just like in a dance, it takes a while for a friendship to develop a rhythm. Just like dancing, it requires paying attention to the other person and watching her or his moves.

Sometimes an up-front comment or question about pacing is appropriate. "I'd love to get together for lunch regularly. Do you have any interest in that? Would it work for you?" "I enjoy playing tennis with you so much. Would it work for you to play more often than we have been?"

Other times, we find ourselves pondering how frequently we should make contact with people we know. How often should I send text messages to friends? Emails? Cards? How often should I phone? Am I doing it too often? Too seldom?

Part of the attraction of online social networking is that we don't have to worry about whether or not we're taking too much initiative in a relationship. We can post comments and links, and watch to see who responds. The process is much less threatening than sending a text message or email to an individual and wondering whether the person we're sending it to really wants to receive it or not.

I find the principles in 1 Corinthians 13 and Colossians 3 to be helpful as I consider how often to make contact with people I know. When I'm feeling anxious about whether or not I should contact a friend, I think about actions toward that friend that would flow out of kindness, compassion and love. Sometimes a supportive email, card or phone call might express kindness and compassion, but sometimes it seems fairly clear that waiting until later would be the kindest or most compassionate thing to do.

Sometimes our ability to be kind and compassionate in a particular friendship simply runs out. Can pulling back from a relationship be consistent with the kind of love God wants for us to experience and express?

PULLING BACK

"Are you going to write about the end of friendships?" Joanne asked me. We were having coffee. I was delighted when she had called the day before to ask me if I had time to meet her. I'd been worried about her for months. In the previous year, she had navigated a couple of extremely hard situations in her work as a human services manager for a hospital. In addition, her son had been diagnosed with a chronic disease.

"Why do you ask?" I responded.

"I've been noticing how I'm stepping out of certain friendships," she replied. She told me about a friend from work who was most comfortable giving and receiving love by doing kind things for others. "I've tried to show her love with actions, but I'm really not very good at that. What I need from friends is words of affirmation, and that friend isn't able to give me those words."

She paused and pondered for a moment. "As I get older, I'm more able to discern which friends will be able to engage in give-and-take with me and which ones feel to me like I'm giving all the time but getting nothing back. Sometimes you have to cut friends loose. With all the stress I've been dealing with, I just don't have the energy to spend on friendships where I feel that I'm giving all the time and they're taking."

Is Joanne being wise and realistic in her choice to let go of a few friendships during this stressful time for her? While I have encouraged reflection on friendship in the light of the love, compassion and kindness expressed in 1 Corinthians and Colossians 3, I also want to assert that no one has an endless supply of those wonderful attributes. At certain times, the right response might very well be to step away from relationships that are draining.

Can stepping away be done in a compassionate and kind way? Gossip can be a very real temptation when we are in the process of moving away from a friend. That friend has become less attractive in our eyes, so it may feel tempting to talk with someone else about that friend's limitations. Keeping compassion and kindness on the front burner, even when making a decision to step away from a friend, limits engagement in destructive practices like gossip.

Joanne might find that in a year, five years or twenty years, some of those neglected friendships will blossom again. Nothing is permanent in friendships. I watched my mother and her brothers become closer friends in their last decades of life, after the death of their mother. I reconnected with my childhood friend Becky after decades of no contact. I've heard story after story of people building bridges many years or even decades after conflicts and estrangement. Love and hope are closely intertwined throughout the New Testament letters of Paul, and love and hope give us optimism, even when relationships seem to be moving apart.

CHOOSING

Friendship involves a constant series of choices. We choose when to initiate and how to respond when others initiate with us. We choose how often to express affection and the way we express it. We choose to give help and to ask for help, and we choose how we respond when help is offered to us. We choose to do things alone, and we choose to do them with friends. We choose to accept or criticize the ways our friends are different from us. We choose to try to forgive when a friend offends us. And the choices mentioned in this paragraph are only a small fraction of the choices we make in friendships.

My younger son believes that one of the most significant choices we make in the area of friendship involves placing ourselves in proximity with people. Proximity, he believes, is the central factor that makes friendships possible. A wide circle of acquaintances provides the pool from which future close friendships develop.

When people criticize Facebook and other forms of social networking as places where superficial relationships are fostered, I find myself wondering why a broad network of relationships with acquaintances would be considered to be a bad thing. As long as a person has some close relationships that are nurtured carefully, having a wide circle of acquaintances is usually enriching and beneficial.

My conviction about the value of acquaintances has been influenced by the research of Mark Granovetter, the author of one of the most quoted academic articles in the field of sociology. Granovetter, a professor at Stanford University, wrote the article in 1973, and much follow-up research has been conducted.

The title of the original article, "The Strength of Weak Ties,"[1] refers to the significance of relationships with acquaintances. Granovetter argues that most people have a few close relationships, or strong ties. In addition, they have a wider circle of acquaintances, which he calls "weak ties," and each of those acquaintances has her or his own circle of close friendships, or strong ties.

Granovetter's research indicates that weak ties, or relationships with acquaintances, are highly productive in creating a healthy society, because weak ties create bridges between networks of close friends. These bridges are essential in communicating information between groups of people, which aids scientific advancement, political discourse, job mobility and many other human endeavors.

In the past two decades, researchers who study online communication have argued that many of the relationships fostered online fall into the category of weak ties. Based on Granovetter's theory, these weak ties are significant in making society work better, because bridges are built between people who would otherwise have no contact with each other. Ideas circulate and percolate, benefiting everyone. Phrases like "I know someone who knows someone" and "a friend of a friend" indicate the way we often draw on people connected to our friends and acquaintances for information, contacts and resources. A large circle of weak ties connects us indirectly to an amazing number of people.

Weak ties—whether they are nurtured online, in the workplace, at church, in the neighborhood or elsewhere—have an additional significance in relation to friendship. A wide circle of acquaintances contains a handful of people with whom deep friendship may one day be possible. According to Granovetter, nurturing a good number of acquaintances provides stimulating connections, which makes life more fruitful and interesting. In addition, acquaintances always have the potential to grow into friends.

Electronic communication is helpful in maintaining contact with acquaintances because it can be so quick and efficient. A rapid-fire email response to a question, a quick online status update, the flick of a text message about an event, a photo sent by cell phone or online—all these can nurture connections among a wide circle of acquaintances. If each of those acquaintances is embedded in a web of close friendships, our connection with those acquaintances gives us some degree of access to many, many close friendship networks with all their attendant resources and knowledge.

Stella, a stay-at-home mom in her thirties, noted that one of the odd outcomes of being on Facebook is that she has developed relationships with people she never desired to connect with. She is bemused by the connections she feels with unexpected people. I feel the same way about Facebook, my congregation and my workplace. Life involves a series of encounters with people with whom I would probably not choose to be connected. In today's world, those encounters happen online as well as in person. Those unexpected, unplanned and sometimes unwelcome crossings of paths result in a circle of acquaintances. Granovetter's research indicates that, for the most part, we are enriched by those connections.

If a person's circle of acquaintances is mostly online, primarily involves a kind of voyeuristic sense of entitlement to information about other people and seldom results in any deepening of relationships, some alarm bells should ring. But if the circle of acquaintances results, from time to time, in the sharing of information and interesting new relational connections, we can be grateful for a range of connections and the benefit they bring. For the sake of future friendships and for the sake of the resources available now, placing a high value on a wide circle of acquaintances makes sense. The challenge is to balance nurturing the larger circle of acquaintances with intentional caring for close friends, making intentional choices to honor both.

CHOOSING FRIENDSHIPS ACROSS GENERATIONS

Several people talked to me about the significance of choosing to nurture friendships across the generations. "One of the best things about friendships is that age doesn't matter," Jeannette said. Retired seven years ago from a teaching position in a university, she has become friends with Joel, who replaced her. Joel is in his thirties, and Jeannette is in her seventies. She said, "He's the same age as my youngest son, but that doesn't seem to matter. We're friends."

Joel is equally grateful for the friendship, even though Jeannette is quite a bit older than his parents.

I couldn't have survived when I first arrived here without Jeannette. She has helped me to understand so many aspects about working in my department and has been very supportive of everything I've done.

Being in different generations takes a lot of things out of

the equation. We're not challenging one another for the same territory at work, for example, and there's no possibility of a romantic relationship. I'm very grateful for my relationship with Jeanette, perhaps to a large extent because there aren't lots of strings attached. Neither of us has an ulterior motive in relation to the other. We enjoy each other's company, enjoy hearing each other's opinions and trust each other.

My mother echoed the same thoughts in a conversation on Valentine's Day. I had called her because I know how much she misses my father on that day. During that phone call, Mom told me that after church that morning, she'd had a conversation with a young couple and their toddler son in the church parking lot. The hus-

Ruth and Naomi: Loyalty and Mentoring

The book of Ruth in the Bible describes a friendship between a foreign woman, Ruth, and her Jewish mother-in-law, Naomi. After Ruth is widowed, Naomi encourages her to stay with her own family, but Ruth wants to go back to Israel with Naomi.

Ruth's words are often quoted in weddings: "Where you go, I will go; where you lodge, I will lodge; your people shall be my people, and your God my God. Where you die, I will die—there will I be buried. May the Lord do thus and so to me, and more as well, if even death parts me from you!" (Ruth 1:16-17).

That kind of loyal love certainly provides a wonderful foundation for a marriage. The friendship between Ruth and Naomi also illustrates the kind of love that sometimes happens between people of different generations. Some people have it in the extended family, with parents or parents-in-law, aunts, uncles, nieces or nephews. Some cross-generational friendships originate at church, in the workplace or in the neighborhood. Ruth was faithful to Naomi, and Naomi mentored Ruth. That combination of loyalty and guidance in friendships across generations is a great gift.

band had wished her a happy Valentine's Day, and she had thanked him, saying it was a day when she particularly missed her husband. The man said, "Tell me more about that," and Mom told him and his wife about some of the things she and my dad had done to celebrate the day.

The couple mentioned that they were going to Hawaii in a few weeks and that they were a bit nervous about leaving their son with his grandparents. My mom then encouraged them to take time for themselves as a couple whenever they could.

When my mom described the conversation to me, she described this young couple as her friends. She has always enjoyed talking to them at church. Mom said, "One of the best things about church is the way it's possible to have friendships across the generations."

Friendship across generations has become less common these days, with extended families scattered across many miles and fewer places where the generations gather. Making intentional effort to build relationships with people of other generations can bring richness and wisdom.

THE IDEAL AND THE REAL

Many of the challenges we experience in pacing and choosing relate to one of Rawlins's friendship dialectics, the tension between the ideal and the real. In our friendships, we have to find a balance point between what we consider to be ideal and what actually happens.

We may wish that we had more friends across the generations, but perhaps those relationships simply aren't happening. Our ideal of friendships with people of all ages may collide with the reality that most of our friends are our age.

Or, in contrast, we may wish that all our friends were similar in age to us so they could understand our age and stage in life. But in reality, some close friends may end up being of a different age, which necessitates that we build bridges across the generations—sometimes a challenging task. And having friends who are quite a bit older can arouse fear of the loss of that friendship with aging and death.

When I was a young adult, I got to know a woman who was almost the same age as my mother. She began as a mentor and guide, and then became a dear friend, my first friend who was my mother's generation instead of my own. My mother is still going strong into her eighties, but this friend died a few years ago, and I miss her still. An ideal friend is a friend for life, but in reality, we lose friends for many reasons, including death.

We may wish we could spend time each week with everyone we care about. But we don't have time to do that. We may hope to stay well connected to close friends, while nurturing connections with a wide circle of acquaintances. In reality, some weeks we do one of those better than the other. We may desire to stay faithful to all our friends, even in times of great stress. But sometimes we have to let go of friendships, at least for a time. We may wish we could initiate with each friend at exactly the right time, but instead we blunder in our friendships, acting when we should have refrained from acting and keeping our distance when we should have reached out and made a connection.

Many people have an inner picture of what a perfect friendship would look like. Unfortunately, nothing can possibly measure up to that golden standard. We are imperfect human beings who engage in imperfect friendships. Each of us has to find a balancing point between the ideals of friendship we long for and the reality of the friendships we have been given.

QUESTIONS FOR REFLECTION, JOURNALING, DISCUSSION OR ACTION

- Spend some time considering the pacing and rhythm of your friendships. What aspects of pacing and rhythm do you think you do well? What aspects could use improvement? Do you feel a pull to make any changes in this area?

- Have you ever had to let a friendship go? What precipitated that decision? Looking back, do you think you did it wisely? Kindly? What have you learned from that decision?

- Where do you connect with acquaintances? In what ways do you nurture relationships with acquaintances? In what ways do you value connections with acquaintances? Spend time pondering the balance between close friends and acquaintances in your life.

- What is your ideal friendship? How do your real friendships compare to that ideal? In what ways do you navigate the tension between the ideal and the real?

- Spend time praying about your friendship patterns in the areas of pacing and choosing, and in the tension between the ideal and the real. Ask God for insight to understand why you do what you do in both areas, and ask for help to grow in these areas.

12

ACCEPTING · FORGIVING

Friends are people who care about you and really listen to you. They pay attention to your life; they know what you are up to. They will be there when you need help. They keep one eye closed to your bad points, and they are good at forgiving.

—Sarah, a life coach in her sixties

A friend is someone you can talk frankly and openly to, and who will not breach your confidence and will not judge you for who you are. They will assume the best intentions in what you do. It takes many years to have a true friend.

—Clara, a teacher in her fifties

My most painful conflict with a friend can be best understood—from my point of view anyway—by considering two of Rawlins's friendship dialectics. Let me begin by explaining what happened.

My friend thought that I was doing numerous things wrong, and one day she told me. She also told me the motivations that she believed lay behind the actions. I agreed that I had done some of the actions, but not all of them. I agreed that some of the actions were inappropriate and unfortunate, but I did not agree that they were as horrible as she seemed to think they were. I did not agree at all with her assessment of my motives for the actions. I was so hurt by the conversation that I was unable to explain my response to her observations with any clarity—although I wrote her a muddled letter that was far too long—and I remained deeply wounded for a long time.

It took years to stop feeling hurt and even more years before I could forgive her. Immediately after the incident, I stepped away from this friendship that had been satisfying and valuable. I didn't want to be friends with someone who would treat me that way.

How much should we accept our friend's flaws without mentioning them? How much should we criticize those flaws? How should that criticism be delivered? One of Rawlins's friendship dialectics illuminates the fact that friends have to find a balance point between judgment and acceptance. I have always erred on the side of acceptance of my friends' flaws. Because friends were so important to me as a child and because criticism always has the potential to damage friendship, I have always been extremely cautious about criticizing friends. The friend who criticized me seemed to have valued a different balance point between acceptance and judgment in friendships.

Another of Rawlins's dialectics came into play as well, the tension between expressiveness and protectiveness. This dialectic addresses the conflict between being honest and hurting a friend's feelings. Honesty in a friendship might involve discussion of a friend's flaws, overlapping with the previous dialectic. But honesty in friendship goes far beyond personal criticism. How do we handle disagreements with friends about politics, religion, culture, lifestyle and everyday choices?

Trust in friendship develops in a kind of dance. We want to believe our friends are being truthful with us, but we also don't like being hurt. So we usually experiment with strategies that preserve honesty while protecting our friend's feelings. I have friends with whom I don't discuss politics, because I don't want to hurt them by disagreeing with them. Again, probably because of my childhood experience with friends, I have usually chosen protectiveness over expressiveness with my friends, tending toward being silent about the things about which I disagree, to protect the friendship.

I simply couldn't handle the conversation with the friend who criticized me. She violated my friendship philosophy and priorities by choosing judgment over acceptance and by choosing expressiveness over protectiveness. I was surprised that some of my interviewees, when asked to define friendship, said they value friends who tell them the truth about what they're doing wrong. Perhaps some of my interviewees would have valued the discussion my friend initiated with me. Perhaps they would have been able to talk rationally about the things my friend was describing. I was so hurt by the conversation that I completely lost my ability to engage productively with the issues my friend had raised.

I now believe, looking back, that the long-term implications of the conflict arose in part from a different understanding of what is appropriate in friendship, specifically in the areas of judgment versus acceptance and expressiveness versus protectiveness. Because of such profound differences on these two dialectics, I believed I would never again be able to trust that friend.

Bella, a financial adviser in her thirties, reflected on the issue of trusting friends when I corresponded with her by email about friendship:

> What I've needed to learn is to be willing to trust people, and to be willing to allow people to rebuild trust. I have ended up with very few lifelong friendships, mostly because when people let me down, I shut them out. But the fact of the matter is, even your friends will let you down sometimes, and you have to give them the chance to rebuild the trust. And that works both ways. Sometimes I let my friends down, and I have to put in the work to re-earn their trust.

Bella's emphasis on viewing friendship as a place where people let each other down then rebuild trust has parallels with Colossians 3:13: "Bear with one another and, if anyone has a complaint against another, forgive each other; just as the Lord has forgiven you, so you also must forgive." I like Bella's emphasis on rebuilding trust as a component of forgiveness.

Bella's words also parallel 1 Corinthians 13:7, which states that love "bears all things, believes all things, hopes all things, endures all things." Love bears with the foibles of friends, even when they have a different balance point on Rawlins's friendship dialectics. Love never gives up believing and hoping that the relationship can be restored.

In my own conflict with a friend, I reached the point where pain and hurt outweighed my ability to love. As a result, I walked away from a friendship that had been valuable to me. I don't know if I could have loved more than I did. But I wish I had been able to do so.

RESTORATION AFTER CONFLICTS
Some friendship conflicts arise from missed communications and unintentional oversights. Glenda, in her seventies, has a close friend from her teen years who lives many miles away. A few years ago, they corresponded by email about the possibility of getting together during the friend's vacation in a neighboring state to the state where Glenda lives. As Glenda remembers it, the friend said she would let Glenda know the details of their vacation.

Several months later, Glenda got a phone call from the friend. "When are you arriving?" Her friend was phoning from the motel where she and her husband were staying in the neighboring state. Glenda was stunned. She thought the vacation must have been canceled, because she hadn't heard any more about it. She tried to explain what had happened as she talked to her friend on the phone, but her friend was angry and wouldn't listen.

A month later, Glenda received a phone call from her friend's daughter, who said that her mother was still deeply hurt by Glenda. Glenda contacted the friend and apologized, but things were still tense between them. Several months later, Glenda's children and her friend's children orchestrated a seventieth birthday party for Glenda, and when the two women met up, their friendship was restored.

Glenda still doesn't know what she could have done differently during the lead-up to the botched vacation gathering, but she is very grateful the relationship has been restored. She's grateful for the help of her children and her friend's children in making the restoration of the relationship possible. We have looked at the significance of initiative in friendship. In this case, much of the initiative for restoring the relationship was taken by Glenda's children and her friend's children, probably the biggest birthday gift Glenda received that year.

Glenda apologized with as much sincerity as she could muster, even though in her mind she hadn't done anything wrong. The friendship was deeply important to her, and she accepted that, if she valued it, she had to take steps to try to restore it.

Glenda's story illustrates the necessity of letting go of hurts and misunderstandings to nurture friendship. It also illuminates one of the ironies of our time. Even with an unprecedented number of ways to stay in touch with people, we still have the capacity to mess up in our communication, to forget to pass along essential information and thus inadvertently to hurt one another.

Boyd, a minister in his sixties, remembers the sweetness of reconciliation with a friend. The incident took place more than thirty-five years ago, and Boyd can't remember the content of the conflict, but he remembers sitting on a park bench talking through it. Boyd said, "When we talked it through rather than avoiding it, we both realized that our friendship had reached a new level. It was based on something deeper than just being compatible." The park bench and the exact setting remain etched in Boyd's mind because of the power of that moment, the time when he learned that conflicts with friends can be resolved, and greater intimacy can result.

Layla, a twenty-year-old student, has experienced that same sweetness of reconciliation. Kimberly, a long-time friend of hers, got into a bad lifestyle. Layla spoke up once or twice about her concern about Kimberly's choices, and Kimberly felt judged. For a year, they didn't talk.

Layla recounted the inner shift that happened, which led to an outer shift as well. "Last year we had a huge breakthrough. I remembered how much I loved her. Nothing we could do could really stop that love. I forgave her in my head, but it was so good to tell her in person. She forgave me in return, and I'm so happy. She is getting married this summer, and I will be in her wedding. We'd talked about our weddings for years, how we'd always be there for each other."

TECHNOLOGY AND RESTORATION OF RELATIONSHIP

Many people have learned the hard way not to engage in conflicts using electronic communication. It is simply too easy to fire off an email or text message when angry. All criticism, confrontation and correction should be done face-to-face if at all possible. A phone call is second best, because at least on the phone we can hear tone of voice and ask questions for clarification.

Can electronic communication play a role in restoration of relationship after a conflict? Yes, with careful attention to the goal of rebuilding trust.

"I have a rule," Bern, a scientist in his fifties, said. "I congratulate people over email but I never castigate them. If I have to confront or correct someone, I always do it in person, or by phone. But recently something happened that helped me see the way email can play a part in resolving a conflict."

Bern walked into a conference room at work, and a colleague from out of town, who Bern knows fairly well, had spread out some papers on a table. Bern noticed a diagram in an unusual shape and made a joke about it. The colleague didn't respond, and other people began to flood into the room.

Later in the week, Bern got an email from the colleague, who by then had returned home. In the email, the colleague explained why he had chosen that shape for the diagram. Bern could tell from the tone of the email that the colleague had been offended by his comment. In his email reply, Bern apologized and indicated his respect for the colleague's work.

That Sunday at Bern's church, the children's sermon included the illustration of a toothpaste tube. The speaker squeezed out a pile of toothpaste, gave the children Popsicle sticks and asked them to put the toothpaste back. When they couldn't do it, she talked about how much easier it is to say words than to take them back.

On Monday, Bern wrote a further email to his colleague. He described the children's message and said that he wished he could take his words back. He said he realized his flippant joke had been hurtful, and he said he was sorry. He explained what he had been thinking when he made the joke.

Bern said emails worked well in this instance because they gave his colleague the opportunity to focus on the topic at hand and to explain clearly what lay behind the diagram. Using emails also gave Bern time to think carefully about the best way to respond and to share what was happening in his life. The email exchange over several days actually strengthened and deepened the relationship.

ASPECTS OF ACCEPTANCE IN FRIENDSHIP

Friendships involve many kinds of acceptance. Bern had to accept that he had offended his colleague unintentionally and that an effort of restoration would be necessary, even though he had not intended to hurt the other man. Glenda had to accept that her friend was deeply hurt, even though she didn't believe she had done anything wrong.

In my childhood, I learned that in order to have friends I had to accept that their interests might be quite different from mine. I learned to engage in their interests in order to be with them, and I found that I grew to appreciate some things I had never before enjoyed.

After moving to New Zealand, I've had to learn to accept the great differences in communication styles among the friends I left behind. Some friends are enthusiastic emailers, and I love hearing from them. Some enjoy Facebook more than email, and Facebook is a growing resource and pleasure for me because it helps me stay connected with those friends. One very dear friend is wrapped up with a baby and a toddler, and I know I will hear from her very seldom. I accept that she values my friendship but simply can't find time to correspond very often. Another close friend simply doesn't communicate with her absent friends. I know that when I see her we'll have a great conversation, but I have to accept that she focuses on her immediate life and not on distant friends.

One of my new friends in New Zealand works in a very intense job. I have to accept that I won't get to see her very often. Another new friend is battling cancer. Obviously our friendship needs to focus on her medical needs for the foreseeable future. I want to support her. I want to be there for her as much as I can be. Her cancer is a great loss for her and a much smaller, but real, loss for me because I have to accept that during the months of chemotherapy and radiation our friendship will be different than it was before her illness.

Job roles contribute significantly to the challenges of acceptance in friendship. When I arrived in New Zealand, the head of my department was one of the people in my workplace with whom I enjoyed talking the most. I had to accept that my friendship with him would have limits, because he was my supervisor.

Stanley, a university professor in his sixties, was recently appointed as president of his institution. Of this shift, he said, "I'm going through a transition now, watching my friendships with colleagues change, of necessity I guess, now that I am president. We still have warm, personal conversations, but positional location makes a difference."

Earlier in his life, Stanley had served in a different supervisory role. "I had good friends there, but there were always boundaries." I suspect that Stanley's colleagues are adjusting to his new role, just as he is, and that they are probably feeling some sadness for

Take a Break from Being Connected

Recently, in the city where I live, a pedestrian was seriously injured in an accident involving a car, a driver and a cell phone. The driver heard the ring announcing an incoming text message and reached over to the passenger seat to pick up the cell phone and glance at the screen. The driver's eyes left the road for just a few seconds too long.

The temptation to stay connected can have disastrous, even deadly results. Oprah has made a pledge never to text while driving. Her pledge is an example of the new kinds of decisions that need to be considered in the midst of all the new ways to communicate.

The temptation to stay connected with people who are not present can disrupt face-to-face relationships. This isn't physically deadly, but it can be deadly in another sense; it can squelch a good conversation and be deadly boring to the person whose cell phone didn't ring. Are you able to ignore text messages that come in while you're talking to someone else? Are you able to refrain from texting friends when you should be paying attention to something or someone else? We have to accept that we simply cannot be connected to everyone every moment.

the changes in the friendship that they will have to accept because of the change in position.

Being supportive and caring for people in a different place on the work hierarchy is a gift of love we can give. But we always have to remember that the difference in position will mean that the friendship will have limits. It will simply not be characterized by complete openness. The same is true with parent-child relationships.

Several people I interviewed talked about the wonderful shifts they have experienced as adults in relation to their own parents. Two women in their thirties talked about moving home for a few months. In those unexpected months, they developed new patterns of relationship with their parents. They became friends.

I asked a group of teenagers if they view their parents as

friends. One responded with laughter, "My parents are great, but they're still parents!" The positional and role issues between parent and child are very different during the teenage years from what they might be in later years. When parents long to develop a friendship with their children, they have to accept that age really does make a difference.

The friendship dialectic mentioned in the previous chapter—the tension between the ideal and the real—comes into play when we consider the many ways acceptance is necessary in friendship. In an ideal world, our friends would have very similar interests to our own, but often they don't, and we have to accept the differences. In an ideal world, presidents of institutions would be able to be close friends with the people they supervise, but in reality, position makes a difference. In an ideal world, children as they grow up would become increasingly closer to their parents as friends, but that often doesn't happen. In an ideal world, siblings would be friends, but in the real world, some sibling relationships are difficult and painful, some are characterized by lack of interest and emotional distance, and a precious few are close and intimate.

We would love to be open, honest and generous with all our friends. In reality, some friends will take too much and other complex issues will arise, so in the real world, boundaries with friends are often necessary.

In an ideal world, we would be able to love people so profoundly that we would be able to forgive and forget quickly and easily in times of conflict. In reality, forgiveness after being hurt by a friend often presents difficulties, and love in challenging relationships is not easy. We can strive for love, pray for it and rely on God to give it to us, but feeling love and acting in love the majority of the time requires a lifetime of learning and commitment.

But we can act with care, compassion and forbearance in friendships as much as possible. And a commitment to acting in love as much as possible will bear very good fruit.

QUESTIONS FOR REFLECTION, JOURNALING, DISCUSSION OR ACTION

- Have you ever had a significant conflict with a friend? What did you learn from it? Have you been able to forgive your friend? Has trust been restored? If not, what do you think it would take to restore that trust?

- When you think about the two friendship dialectics discussed in this chapter—acceptance versus judgment and expressiveness versus protectiveness—how do you see those tensions playing out in your current friendships?

- In your closest friendships, what are the hardest things for you to accept? What helps you accept them?

- Spend some time meditating on 1 Corinthians 13 and Colossians 3:12-17. In what ways do they challenge you as you engage in friendships? In what ways do they affirm your friendship practices?

- This week, ask two or three friends, colleagues or acquaintances what they think is the role of forgiving and accepting in friendship. What do you agree with or disagree with in their comments?

- Spend time praying about your friendship patterns in the area of accepting and forgiving. Ask God for insight to understand why you do what you do, and ask God for help to grow in these areas. If there is a friend you need to forgive, ask for God's help to do so. If you have hurt a friend, spend some time confessing what you did wrong. Ask for God's wisdom and strength to seek to rebuild trust.

13

A FRIENDSHIP EXPERIMENT

My closest friends, perhaps you'd call them my soul mates, are my husband and my mother. There is no one else I'm fonder of and to whom I can regularly open up my heart without fear. There are circles of relationships in my life that radiate out from there, and I am fond of them and trust them and share with them—more or less. To label them all as "friends" seems to cheat the word a little bit. Maybe we need several categories of friendship: acquaintances, buddies, friends, soul mates.

—Louise, a musician in her fifties

The words friend *and* friendship *bring to mind deep sharing, deep listening, intimacy, a sense of ease, willingness to risk in care and concern, joy, laughter, fun, jokes, kidding, different levels with different folks and different friends for different times . . . but all good.*

—Jack, a university professor in his fifties

At age twenty-two, I moved to Seattle. I lived there until I was fifty-five, except for three years abroad at ages twenty-six, twenty-seven and thirty-three.

In the thirty years I lived in Seattle, I practiced the intentional habits described in this book. I took initiative with people over and over. I made phone calls, arranged get-togethers, sent emails and cards, and hosted hundreds of dinners in my home. I asked for help when I needed it, and I asked for prayer support frequently. I made a real effort to grow in my ability to listen carefully to people.

I put myself in places where people gather. I went to church almost every Sunday for those thirty-plus years. In the first decade in Seattle, I attended a weekly couple's home group and a weekly mom's group, then in the second decade a weekly women's Bible study group and in the third decade two monthly prayer support groups and a book group. I tried to be open to new relationships and to welcome new people in our neighborhood and at church. I tried to befriend work colleagues.

I tried to be a faithful friend.

The fruit of these intentional practices was fantastic. Friends. Many friends. Rich and wonderful friends. My friends helped me through difficult challenges: depression, toddlers, teenagers, several serious illnesses and the transition to working after being at home.

When we moved to New Zealand three year ago, I decided to try something different. It was my second friendship experiment. I had engaged in a friendship experiment in high school, which proved to be a great learning experience, even though the immediate effects were mostly disastrous (see chapter five).

If my friendship habits in Seattle were working so well and if my previous friendship experiment was not a success, why would I try another experiment now?

INTROVERTS AND EXTROVERTS IN FRIENDSHIP

Some of the motivation for my second friendship experiment came from conversations with my brother, Mark, about his friendship patterns. He is a congenial, easygoing man who considers himself to be an introvert. He has a tight circle of close friends, most of them in the city where he has lived for thirty years. He met two of his friends in high school, one in college and several more in his early adult years.

Mark has made intentional choices to limit his close friendships to those few. He has tried to be a faithful friend to that handful of men, supporting them through illnesses, job transitions, family challenges and divorces. Mark works full time, and he enjoys spending time with his wife and kids. It takes all the relational energy he has to do his job, love his family and spend time with his small circle of friends.

People often reach out to him in friendship, and he is friendly and cordial to them, but he does not take steps to include them in his tight circle of friends. The reality of his life is that he is stretched relationally as much as he desires to be. He doesn't want to do more.

A conversation with another friend influenced my recent friendship experiment as well. Connie, an occupational therapist in her fifties, said she is often struck by the fact that so many women talk about having a "best friend." Connie's best friend is her husband.

"I'm an introvert," she noted. "I only need one best friend." She is delighted to have a handful of women friends in her life, but she doesn't look to one of them to be a "best friend." She is very aware of the limits of her energy for people, and she stewards it well, focusing most deeply on her husband and then using the rest of it to do her job and maintain a small circle of other friends.

My mother, who is an extrovert, is able to sustain an amazingly large circle of friends. She has never met someone who isn't a candidate for friendship. She is realistic that some relationships won't develop into friendships, but she is open to friendship with anyone she meets. She knows the skills of friendship and she uses them frequently. I grew up with my mother's strong influence as a friendship model.

My own dislike of being lonely every time we moved during my childhood has also shaped me. I feel safer and more secure when I have friends. Making and nurturing friendships has always been a significant priority for me.

When we left Seattle three years ago, I looked back on my years there. I realized I had taken it too far. I simply didn't have the energy necessary to sustain all the friendships I had developed. My friends were—and are—so precious that I couldn't ignore them. I didn't want to ignore them. Living in the same city as many of my friends meant that I continually felt the desire to get together with them and to encourage them when they needed support.

I'm an introvert. I am an unusual introvert in that I am quite talkative, but I am definitely energized by the inner life, the central characteristic of introversion. Typically introverts have fewer, deeper friendships than extroverts. I was living like an introvert in that I valued and nurtured deep friendships. Yet I was also living like an extrovert in that I valued and nurtured caring relationships with a wide circle of close friends. It was too much.

When we moved to New Zealand, I decided to scale down my exercise of the intentional friendship skills I have described in this book. I cut back on the initiative I had taken to get together with women for lunches or coffee. I didn't join any small groups for the first year, and in the second year I joined a group for a few months then gradually drifted away. I had never done that in my life. I had always followed through with my commitments to people and to groups.

I found that my friendship with my husband flourished. He had always been my closest friend, but now he is much closer than anyone else nearby. We share more deeply than we ever have before, and we depend on each other more. I find my increased dependence on him to be a bit scary. If he dies before I do, I will be lonelier than I would have been during our years in Seattle, when I was surrounded by so many close friends.

I've kept in contact with American friends in a variety of ways: emails, letters, cards, phone calls and Facebook. Sometimes I desperately miss my friends in Seattle. Other times I'm grateful that the distance has created a dilution of some of the friendships, because I can see more clearly now that I am not cut out for having dozens of close friendships.

BEFRIENDING LONELINESS

Despite my close friendship with my husband, and despite the numerous ways of staying in contact with friends in the United States, I've experienced in New Zealand more loneliness over a longer period of time than ever before in my life. I have made a conscious effort to focus on Jesus as my Friend in those instances. What I miss about my close friends is the deep understanding they gave me. I remind myself that Jesus understands me even better than they do, and he longs to listen to me even more intensely than they do.

Alone Versus Lonely

I was talking to a group of seven teenagers, ages sixteen to nineteen. I told them I experience a significant difference between being alone and feeling lonely. They all nodded.

Ed, eighteen, said, "When you feel lonely, you know you're emotionally missing something."

Emma, sixteen, said, "Being alone feels fine when you know you could be with someone or talking to someone, but you're not."

Mark, sixteen, agreed with Emma. "Being alone is a choice. When you don't have a choice, you're more likely to feel lonely."

Emma added, "But being lonely can be a choice as well. It can be the result of the choices you've made not to stay connected to people."

It can be fruitful to ponder the variety of emotions connected with being contentedly alone versus feeling lonely. I've tried to grow in viewing the feeling of loneliness as a call to draw closer to God, my true Friend. I've also tried to be thankful that feeling lonely indicates how profoundly human beings were created for relationships. God in three persons is a God of relationship, inviting us into the intimacy between Father, Son and Holy Spirit. When we feel lonely, we are experiencing lack of intimacy, a sign of the brokenness of this poor world where we live.

After three years here, I have developed a small number of friendships despite the fact that I slowed down my efforts to make friends. Some people have persisted in initiating with me, and I have responded. My work colleagues gather for lunch every Friday, a pattern they had developed long before I arrived, and I have grown in friendship with those workmates. And, after a lifetime of initiating continually with friends, I found I couldn't stop entirely. I simply slowed down the pace of initiating, so friendships have developed more slowly than earlier in my life, but they have developed anyway. My New Zealand friends are wonderful, and I'll enjoy seeing where these friendships go in the years to come.

My friendship experiment has had the unintentional effect of bringing some delayed healing for the pain of loneliness from my childhood. I can see more clearly that my profound dislike of loneliness after all those moves made me a bit compulsive about finding and making friends. I've let go of some of that compulsiveness. I've befriended loneliness in a new way, finding more peace in it.

My recent friendship experiment has also laid the foundation for the remaining decade or two of my work life. I have less energy than I had when I was younger. As long as my work remains a priority for me, I will need to steward that energy more carefully than I needed to do when I was younger. I cannot engage in as many activities with friends as I used to and retain enough energy for work. I need to befriend loneliness in a new way, and I need to be more careful in nurturing friendships, in order to steward the energy I've been given.

Electronic communication is a fantastic gift at this time in my life when I want to stay in touch with a lot of people in the most efficient way possible. Some of my friends are far away, and electronic means of communication are the only way to connect. But even with the new friends in the city where I now live, electronic connections enable me to stay in touch while spacing out the longer, more intimate, face-to-face connections. Like everyone else in these busy times, I have to consider carefully how best to use the finite energy and time I have been given, and electronic forms of communication help me do it.

Befriending loneliness more intentionally has been a healthy spiritual endeavor for me. When I'm honest, I can look back on those years in Seattle when I had a lot of close friends, and I can see that I experienced some degree of loneliness even then. Despite having a good marriage. Despite having friends. I've come to believe that feelings of loneliness are inevitable for me and perhaps for many other people as well, because we were created for an unbroken relationship with God and with the people around us. And we simply don't have either one.

Human sin and brokenness mar our ability to see God clearly: "For now we see in a mirror, dimly. . . . Now [we] know only in part" (1 Corinthians 13:12). Because we can't see and know God

What We've Gained, What We've Lost

A close friend from Seattle and I have kept in touch for the past three years through emails, phone calls and one precious visit. Recently she took a vacation to Hawaii, her first trip with a laptop along. She emailed several times, the first time asking for an update about a little medical issue I had been experiencing and telling me about the book she read on the plane. Later she described sightseeing trips and snorkeling. She sent a dramatic photo of a humpback whale breaching and asked for prayer when her husband felt sick.

I felt so close to her on that vacation. The immediacy I felt paralleled the experience of the teenagers I interviewed, who talked about staying connected to their friends in the midst of everyday events through text messages and Facebook. Most of the teenagers I interviewed spoke enthusiastically about the value of these numerous brief connections. They experience being a part of each other's lives, even when they are not physically present with each other.

Two of the big friendship challenges of our time—busyness and mobility—have created distance between friends. Electronic communication, when used intentionally, can restore some of that lost connection. It can provide an immediacy that nurtures intimacy if the electronic communication is part of a broader, loving friendship.

fully yet, we can't experience the full relationship with God we were created for. In Christ, we have the enormous blessing of restored intimacy with God, but the connection is still not full and complete. We still see the light in a reduced form, as in a mirror. On Earth, some degree of loneliness seems to be inevitable, given the dimness of our vision that keeps us from complete intimacy with God.

Human sin and brokenness also limit our ability to see clearly and connect deeply with others, further insurance that some feelings of loneliness are inevitable. Human sin and brokenness inhibit our ability to be at peace within ourselves. As a result, we often feel lonely when we are alone. In fact, we can also feel lonely when we are with other people, when the connection with them isn't what we would like it to be.

Yet, despite our moments of loneliness, the Holy Spirit is at work building bridges between people and between people and God. Acts of friendship participate in God's reversal of the powers of alienation at work in our world. When we listen carefully, when we reach out to someone in an act of love, when we choose to try to renew trust after it has been broken, we are taking part in God's work of reconciliation.

Every act of friendship, large or small, builds a bridge. Every act of loving friendship brings healing balm to this broken world. Small gestures like passing on a compliment or sending a postcard, and large sacrificial deeds like flying across country to help a friend after a surgery, are like stones in a bridge linking people together. Or they might be considered to be squares in a beautifully handcrafted quilt. The quilt of friendship keeps us warm on cold winter days.

Every act of friendship, whether it is well received or not, transforms us into people who know a little bit more about love, who understand a little bit more deeply what it means to be a neighbor to the people around us. Friendship transforms us, even as it brings healing, reconciliation and warmth to the world.

QUESTIONS FOR REFLECTION, JOURNALING, DISCUSSION OR ACTION

- Have you ever engaged in a friendship experiment? What did you do, and what did you learn from it? Would you like to engage in an experiment in any form right now?

- Do you consider yourself to be an extrovert or an introvert? How does that characteristic influence the way you conduct your friendships?

- In which situations do you experience loneliness? How do you typically cope with it? Which of your coping strategies do you view as healthy and productive, and which of them have destructive elements? What would you like to change in your patterns of dealing with feelings of loneliness?

- Ask one or two of your friends what they most appreciate about you as a friend. Tell them what you most appreciate about them as a friend.

- Spend some time praying about your patterns of friendship in any of the ways that have been illuminated by this book. Ask God for insight to understand why you do what you do, and ask for help to grow in these areas.

APPENDIX

Discussion and Reflection Questions
About Other Friendship Topics

In this book, I've covered topics about friendship that I care about deeply, topics about which I have strong opinions and topics for which I have stories that illustrate and illuminate the points I wanted to make. Numerous other topics have not been covered.

If you've used this book in a small-group discussion, you may want to continue talking about friendship even though the book has ended. If you've enjoyed reflecting on your own patterns of friendship as you've read this book, you may desire to continue with more journaling or pondering. If either of these scenarios is true for you, below are a few discussion and reflection questions on some of the topics that have not been covered in this book.

GROUPS OF FRIENDS

- Do you have some friends whom you see most often in group settings rather than one-on-one? If so, how do you believe relationships within a group differ from one-on-one relationships? What kinds of relational patterns can happen in a group but not in a one-on-one relationship?

- What do you consider to be the biggest challenges in nurturing friendships with a group of friends? What are the biggest gifts of having a group of friends?

- Do you find some one-on-one contact to be necessary with friends, even if you mostly gather with them in a group? If so, what do you think happens in a one-on-one setting that cannot happen in a group?

- If you could change one thing about the relationships or the patterns of communication in your group of friends, what would it be? Why might you want to change it? How might you take steps to begin to change it?

- Colossians 3:12-17 was written to a group of people, not to an individual. Spend time meditating on the various components in these verses. Consider bringing one verse or even one idea from the passage to your group of friends for discussion and possible implementation.

FRIENDSHIPS BETWEEN MEN AND WOMEN

- Do you believe close friendships are possible between men and women who are not romantically involved with each other? Have you experienced such friendships?

- What are the blessings of close friendships between men and women? What are the hazards?

- If someone younger than you came to ask your advice about a friendship with a person of the opposite sex, what would you say?

- What sorts of boundaries or guidelines are helpful in close friendships between men and women? What boundaries or guidelines are necessary? Why?

- If you have a close friendship with someone of the opposite sex, are there boundaries or guidelines you need to implement? What would it look like to implement those boundaries or guidelines right now?

- If you have a close friendship with someone of the opposite sex, how could you pray about that relationship in new ways? Pray through Colossians 3:12-17 with that friendship in mind.

FRIENDSHIPS WITHIN MARRIAGE

- Do you believe marital partners can be each other's closest friends? Do you believe they should be? Do you believe such friendship often happens within marriage? Why or why not?

- What do you think are the greatest obstacles to a close friendship between partners?

- What do you think married couples can do to nurture friendship with their spouses? What have you observed couples do that seems to work well?

- If you are married, what do you already do to foster friendship with your partner? What might you do that you don't do now? Think of one act of friendship that you might do this week with your spouse.

- If you are not married, what might you do in a dating or engagement relationship to foster friendship with the other person?

- Spend some time praying through 1 Corinthians 13 as it applies to your marriage or dating relationships.

FRIENDSHIPS WITHIN THE FAMILY AND EXTENDED FAMILY

- When you think of your relationships with your immediate and extended family members, which people would you call friends as well as relatives? What helped you grow in friendship with those individuals?

- Do you think family members should be friends as well as relatives? Why or why not?

- Have you experienced shifts toward closer friendship with family members? What made those shifts happen?

- When you think of people within your immediate or extended family who you would not call friends, how do you feel? What are the obstacles to friendship with those family members? Does it seem that those obstacles are insurmountable? Why or why not?

- Many people think of their pets as their friends or members of their family. What do you think and feel about this practice? What are the forces at work in human nature and human society that make relationships with animals attractive and sometimes quite helpful? What would be the defining characteristics that make a friendship with a pet healthy or unhealthy?

- If you could pray for one thing in your relationships within your immediate or extended family, what would it be? If you could take one action this week to express love and care to a family member, what would it be?

- Spend some time meditating on 1 Corinthians 13 or Colossians 3:12-17, asking for God's help to apply the passage in your family.

FRIENDSHIPS IN THE WORKPLACE

- When you think about the people in your workplace, would you consider any of them friends? What has contributed to making the friendship possible?

- What boundaries or limits do you think are necessary when developing a friendship with a workmate? What have you learned about helpful limits on gossip in the workplace?

- Do you have friends at work who are at different levels of the work hierarchy than you are? What makes those friendships work? What are the limits to the friendships?

- If someone came to you to ask advice about making friends in the workplace, what would you say?

- Spend some time reflecting on 1 Corinthians 13 or Colossians 3:12-17 as they relate to your ability to reflect God's love in the workplace. What is one thing you might do this week to show love for someone in your workplace?

FRIENDSHIPS WITH PEOPLE OF DIFFERENT RELIGIOUS OR FAITH COMMITMENTS

- Have you ever experienced a friendship with someone who belongs to a different religion than you do or has a different faith commitment than you do? What were or are the blessings of that friendship? What were or are the challenges?

- Do you believe it is appropriate in a friendship to try to convince the other person that she or he should consider your faith or religion? Why or why not?

- What guidelines do you think are appropriate in discussing faith or religion with someone who has different beliefs than you have? Do you find it easy or hard to practice those guidelines? What are the factors that make it easy or hard?

- If you could change one thing about your own patterns of communication as you engage in friendships with people of different faith or religious commitments, what would it be?

- Spend some time praying through 1 Corinthians 13, keeping in mind your friends with differing religious or faith commitments. What is one thing you might do this week to show love in one of those relationships?

FRIENDSHIP AND FOOD

- Think about your friendship patterns as they relate to food and drink as ways of connecting with others. What do you like about the patterns you notice in your life? What do you think is not healthy? What role do you think food and drink can play in life-giving friendships?

- Look back over your life and notice the times and places when people have offered hospitality to you in their homes. In what ways has that hospitality nurtured friendship? What have you learned from the hospitality of others?

- In what ways do you exercise hospitality? What are the obstacles in your life to offering hospitality? In what new ways would you like to offer hospitality to friends or potential friends? Think of one way you could exercise hospitality in the next week or two.

- Spend some time meditating on Colossians 3:12-17, considering the ways the principles in the passage overlap with your experiences of hospitality and your patterns related to food and drink in friendships. Write out a prayer of thanks. Continue the prayer, asking God for guidance, wisdom and strength to apply the principles of Colossians 3 to your friendships.

BOUNDARIES IN FRIENDSHIP

- Boundaries are the limits we place in relationships that keep us from becoming manipulated by others or emotionally enmeshed with them. What are some examples of boundaries you have established in your friendships? What are examples of boundaries you need to establish?

- What do you find difficult about establishing and maintaining boundaries with friends? What do you find fairly easy about boundaries? What are some of the causes of the ease and/or difficulty you experience?

- What emotions do you feel about the boundaries you have established or should establish with friends? What patterns in your childhood or in your beliefs about God might contribute to these feelings?

- Read 1 Corinthians 13 and ponder the connections between boundaries and love. What connections can you see? If the love described in 1 Corinthians is best manifested in Jesus, what boundaries do you believe he exercised?

- Write out a prayer about boundaries in your friendships, asking for God's wisdom and help.

NOTES

Chapter 1: Real Relationships

[1]"The medium is the message," Marshall McLuhan asserted in 1967 in the book with the same title. Neil Postman made a similar argument in 1985 in *Amusing Ourselves to Death* (New York, Penguin, 2005, twentieth anniversary edition).

[2]Heidi Campbell is the author of two significant books that explore the way religious communities use the Internet and other new communication technologies: *When Religion Meets New Media* (London: Routledge, 2010) and *Exploring Religious Community Online* (New York: Peter Lang, 2005). The opinions attributed to Dr. Campbell in these two paragraphs come from interviews with her by the author, November 14–18, 2009.

[3]The comments I heard in interviews resemble the "third-person effect," documented by many scholars, in which individuals believe that media have more negative influence on others than on themselves. People believe they can handle violence or pornography, but that others will not be able to cope as well (for example, W. P. Davison, "The Third-Person Effect in Communication," *Public Opinion Quarterly* 47, no. 1 [1983]: 1-15).

Chapter 2: Friendship Then and Now

[1]"Bowling Alone: America's Declining Social Capital," *Journal of Democracy* 6, no. 1 (January 1995): 65-78.

[2]Robert Putnam, *Bowling Alone* (New York: Simon and Schuster, 2000).

[3]Miller McPherson, Lynn Smith-Lovin and Matthew E. Brashears, "Social Isolation in America: Changes in Core Discussion Networks over Two Decades," *American Sociological Review* 71, no. 3 (June 2006): 353-75.

[4]C. S. Lewis, *The Four Loves* (London: Geoffrey Bles, 1960), pp. 69-70.

Chapter 4: Challenges from Technology

[1]Claude Fischer, in *America Calling: A Social History of the Telephone to 1940* (Berkeley: University of California Press, 1992), reflects on the rapid shifts in social life in only a few decades: "In 1875 Americans who wanted to

send a message had to travel or use an intermediary who traveled; the messages were brief and one-way; the range and volume of communication were severely limited. (Use of the telegraph was highly restricted to business and rare emergencies.) In 1925 most Americans could speak to one another across town or across the country quickly, back and forth, and fully. The possibilities of personal communication expanded vastly" (p. 23). Fischer calls this a "drastically new condition of social life," which has interesting parallels with the rapid communication changes in the past two decades.

[2]Ibid., p. 3.
[3]Ibid., p. 1.

Chapter 5: Challenges Beyond Technology

[1]The article by Miller McPherson, Lynn Smith-Lovin and Matthew E. Brashears cited earlier, "Social Isolation in America: Changes in Core Discussion Networks over Two Decades," *American Sociological Review* 71, no. 3 (June 2006): 353-75, documents this trend.

[2]Ezra Klein, "Why I Didn't Love 'I Love You, Man,'" *The American Prospect*, www.prospect.org/csnc/blogs/ezraklein_archive?month=04&year=2009 &base_name=why_i_didnt_love_i_love_you_ma (accessed May 10, 2009).

Chapter 6: Friendship with God

[1]Stanley J. Grenz, in *Rediscovering the Triune God: The Trinity in Contemporary Theology* (Minneapolis: Fortress Press, 2004), uses the words *renaissance* and *rebirth* to describe the rise in interest in trinitarian theology in the twentieth century. He goes on to say, "By the end of the twentieth century, the concept of relationality had indeed moved to center stage. In fact, the assumption that the most promising beginning point for a viable trinitarian theology lies in the constellation of relationships among the three trinitarian persons had become so widely accepted that it attained a kind of quasi-orthodox status" (p. 112).

Chapter 7: Initiating

[1]Abraham and Sarah's story of infertility is told in Genesis 15–21, and Hannah's story is told in 1 Samuel 1 and 2.

[2]Gary D. Chapman's best-known book is probably *The Five Love Languages: How to Express Heartfelt Commitment to Your Mate* (Chicago: Northfield Publishing, 1995). Chapman has written numerous other books about the five love languages in the family and for children.

Chapter 9: Asking • Giving • Thanking

[1]David Steindl-Rast, *Gratefulness, the Heart of Prayer* (New York: Paulist Press, 1984), pp. 15-16.

[2]Ibid., p. 17.

Chapter 10: Sharing • Caring • Being Together • Being Apart

[1]"Lovers are normally face-to-face, absorbed in each other; Friends, side by side, absorbed in some common interest." C. S. Lewis, *The Four Loves* (London: Geoffrey Bles, 1960), p. 73.

[2]William K. Rawlins, *Friendship Matters: Communication, Dialectics and the Life Course* (Hawthorne, N.Y.: Aldine, 1992).

Chapter 11: Pacing • Choosing

[1]Mark Granovetter, "The Strength of Weak Ties," *American Journal of Sociology* 78, no. 6 (May 1973): 1360-80.

ABOUT THE AUTHOR

After years of church ministry in Seattle, Washington, as a Presbyterian minister, Lynne M. Baab completed a Ph.D. in communication at the University of Washington in 2007 and moved with her husband to Dunedin, New Zealand, where she is a lecturer in pastoral theology at the University of Otago.

Books and Bible Studies by Lynne Baab

Visit www.ivpress.com for more information on the following books and Bible studies.

Sabbath Keeping

978-0-8308-3258-3

"Not just a gentle and informative introduction to sabbath; it is an inspiration. Without question, this is the best book I've read in years on the art and discipline of keeping sabbath."

Lauren Winner, author, *Girl Meets God*

Fasting

978-0-8308-3501-0

"*Fasting: Spiritual Freedom Beyond Our Appetites* packs a surprising amount of content. . . . [W]ill help novice Christians dip in . . . and more seasoned practitioners become more creative and intentional."

Publishers Weekly, starred review

Prayers of the Old Testament

978-0-8308-3138-8

Eight studies, based on prayers from seven Old Testament books, invite you to meet our mighty, loving God in fresh ways.

Prayers of the New Testament
978-0-8308-3137-1

In these Bible studies you'll find new words and new ways to pray through the prayers of Mary, Simeon and Anna, Peter, Paul, John and Jesus himself.

Sabbath
978-0-8308-3134-0

The studies in this guide will help you to learn more about what sabbath is—a gift from God that brings a renewed awareness of who God is and who we are as God's beloved children—and how to practice it.

To interact with Lynne and to
keep up with her writing and other activities,
visit her website: www.lynnebaab.com.